Ashes in the Closet

Sandra Still and Elizabeth M. Roberts

ISBN 979-8-88685-844-0 (paperback)
ISBN 979-8-88685-845-7 (digital)

Christian Faith Publishing
832 Park Avenue
Meadville, PA 16335
www.christianfaithpublishing.com

Printed in the United States of America

Disclaimer

I have tried to recreate events, locales, and conversations from my memories of them. In order to maintain their anonymity, in some instances, I have changed the names of individuals and places. Also, I may have changed some identifying characteristics and details such as physical properties, occupations, and places of residence.

To all those who have had life turn their dreams and efforts into ashes, only to realize in time that God has brought beauty, hope, and goodness from sorrows. May God continue to bless them, keep them, and walk beside them, whispering, "Fear not, for I am with you."

To bestow on them a crown of beauty instead of
ashes, the oil of joy instead of mourning, a garment
of praise instead of a spirit of despair.

—Isaiah 61:3

Contents

Introduction

Tell me, please. When do these promises of beauty, joy, and praise begin? Authoring this book of meditations has proven to be a great challenge, an exercise in procrastination, because many of the stories and poems hurt too much. We—Elizabeth and I—didn't want to revisit the events. We didn't want to feel the emotions, hurts, and loneliness.

The irony is that when we look at our present lives, we recognize God's provision and know we are incredibly blessed. We know that God has and does bring beauty, joy, and praise out of the difficult experiences that leave us, even yet, with traces of sorrow. Or if not sorrow, that remind us of life's negative side. Along with great appreciation and gratitude there lies this lump of heaviness, of sadness.

Life often can seem to be one long sorrow, especially in light of the past COVID-19, years. We have endured the seemingly endless divisions among the peoples of our nation and our world. There are too many ashes in the closet, literally and figuratively. Too many bodies on the ground. Too much separation and loss. Too much evil, sadness, deception, illness, and pain. It can easily drive us to despair—or more hopefully—to our knees in prayer to the Lord where, in his great mercy and love, he meets us.

Jesus knew sorrow. His family knew aching sadness. Mary was early on warned that her heart would be pierced with grief, and this warning culminated in her watching her innocent son die in agony on a cross. Yes, he gloriously arose from the grave in triumph, and Mary was eventually awed in joyfulness. But one wonders. Were the horrible memories, seared on her brain, ever truly forgotten in her lifetime?

It seems that even when a difficult situation eventually turns out well, unexpected emotions arise without our bidding, sabotaging our joy. Fortunately, as time passes, joy hopefully grows stronger as we begin to better understand and see how all things work together for good for those who love the Lord. However, at least for us, it seems a slow process, full of ups and downs. While the ashes may still remain in the closet, literally or figuratively, with the Lord's constant presence assisting us, we will be able to courageously live the rest of our lives according to his will.

In this series of meditative stories, we will explore life's hurtful events with a focus on how the Lord weaves them into a tapestry of beauty, hope, and joy. And let us be ever mindful that this world is not our home. Never, here, will we understand or make sense of it all, but in our true home, in God's kingdom, all will be incredibly beautiful and good. Come, Lord Jesus!

Ashes in the Closet

Give thanks to the Lord in all circumstances, for
this is the will of God in Christ Jesus for you.
—1 Thessalonians 5:18

His ashes from the cremation are in a sturdy box in the closet, three shelves down from the top. Right there, right beside the important papers file box. Seems a fitting place, at least for the foreseeable future. Now and again, I ask myself, "What are my future plans regarding this?" Honestly, I have no idea. Burial in the backyard of our former house, where we lived together for thirtysome years, seems most fitting. However, I really can't walk up to the front door and ask the new owners, "Can I bury my husband's remains in your backyard, the place he loved so much?"

He never lived at my new home because he was at the nursing home under hospice as I did a very necessary downsize and relocated a half mile away from our former large house. Interring him here, in a place he had never visited or lived at, doesn't seem fitting either. Perhaps someday a memorial park? With no family here, and his friends drifting away as time goes by, once I'm gone, no one would visit the grave site to shed tears and share memories. Guess for now it's the closet. Ashes in the closet.

Never, in my or most anyone else's wildest imaginings, would such a life-disrupting pandemic, COVID-19, have been fathomable. My husband had been steadily declining for several years to the point where full-time nursing care at a facility was the only option. Increasingly frequent falls at home, and my inability to safely move him from bed to wheelchair, made the decision easier for both of us. Given the circumstances, the nursing home proved tolerable. He seemed happy there, and the care was excellent. A few days after he had gotten settled in, he told me, "I'm fine with being here. I finally feel safe." Treasured words to my aching heart.

Located very close to my home, the facility was easy to visit. Most every day, at some point, I stopped by, often bringing our dog, Calvin, along to visit "Dad." With one of his favorite television shows on, my husband enjoyed sharing time with us. Me sitting at the bedside while Calvin snuggled up on the bed. Always, I'd bring a treat of some sort, and we had quiet, calm time together.

In early March of 2020, the nursing facility went into COVID quarantine, as did so many others. The pandemic had struck the nation and keeping nursing home staff and patients safe and uninfected became essential. No visitors allowed. None. I saw him on a Tuesday evening; they phoned Wednesday and said visiting is no longer allowed. Sadly, I joined other people standing outside who tapped on windows, hoping to get their loved one's attention. Every now and then, my husband would be awake, look at the window, and smile, waving. Usually, however, he was asleep and unresponsive. Other visitors and I would smile at each other through our shared sorrow, hearts grieving, and then trudge back to our cars. There was nothing to be done and little to say.

The dreary month wore on, the pandemic worsened, and my husband declined. Early in April, the facility's hospice director phoned me. "You need to come visit your loved one. He is shutting down, and we feel he'll slip away in a day or two. We want you to be able to say goodbye and to assure him it is okay for him to let go."

The phone call no one ever wants to hear. Upon arrival at the appointed time, I was gowned, masked, and ushered into his room. His roommate had been taken out, and I was allowed to take the mask off. Quietly, I shut the door and walked over to see him for the first time in a month. While fairly unresponsive, I could tell he knew I was there when I took his hand and gently stroked his face. How tired he looked—how worn and tired. He had enough strength to give my hand a gentle squeeze when I asked if he knew who I was, though his eyes were closed.

"Jesus loves you," I sang. A slight smile appeared on his face. He rested quietly as I sang several other of his favorite hymns. "Sweetheart," I said in as strong a voice as I could muster, "I know you are so, so tired out. It's okay to go home to the Lord. It's okay to let go and rest in Jesus. When He comes for you, just go on. I'll join you someday. You've been a good, good husband, and I love you. Despite hard times now and again, I love you. I love you very, very much. You're a good man, and you are loved by many. Especially by me."

As the allotted time peacefully passed by, he fell asleep while I held his hand and continued to stroke his forehead. When the hospice volunteer came in, I masked up and slipped out of the room. To me, it had been a long, long month without seeing him, but the volunteer gently said, "Ma'am, he has no time sense. To him, you've been by his side every moment as he remembers you now. He's not been distressed."

I cling to that. The next day, my husband quietly slipped away and went to be with the Lord. Ashes to ashes, dust to dust. Life on this Earth is brief and fleeting. A person is here today and then gone tomorrow. They take a breath, and then they don't take another one. My husband is with the Lord, and I shall join him someday, but for now, life has forever altered. God's children are with Him for all eternity; therein lies our hope.

Beauty for Ashes

1. Spend some quiet time reflecting on a deeply difficult, life-changing time in your life. What was it? How have you handled the event and its aftermath?

2. Consider the concept of "eternity." What does that word mean to you? How do you visualize "life for eternity?"

Scripture Reflection: "Give thanks to the Lord in all circumstances, for this is the will of God in Christ Jesus for you" (1 Thess. 5:18).

How is it possible to give thanks to the Lord in all circumstances? Why do you think God admonishes us to do this?

Prayer Thought: "Father, our grand and glorious God, many of life's hurts are beyond our ability to understand. In your mercy, lead us into acceptance, peace, and ever-increasing trust in You, even when life seems to hurt too much to bear. For You, Lord, will make all things new and comfort your children. Amen."

Together

The ashes in my closet
remind me daily of you.
The stranger who became my friend,
my confidante, my biggest fan.

You always had my back.
We loved, we laughed.
We even cried in the
good times and the bad.

We stood together
side by side
knowing what we had.
The Lord brought us together
to help each other through,
this life we lived together,

Together, me and you.

Elizabeth M. Roberts

Wheel on In

"That which goes down usually must go up." Wheelchair ramps tend to have one intrinsic drawback. They slope. Those who propel themselves in a wheelchair, and those caregivers who push others in a wheelchair, know exactly the issues stated in that quote.

"Before your husband can go home," the rehabilitation facility social worker told me, "you'll need to purchase a sturdy wheelchair. While he can get around in the house with a walker, he can't safely walk very far. Since you'll be taking him to doctors' appointments and probably other places, you'll need wheels. Once you purchase one, bring it here and his physical therapist will work with him and you on how to use it safely."

I nodded slowly, somewhat in shock. One doesn't buy a wheelchair very often; where did I even begin? I drove home, went into the house, and suddenly a startling realization hit. I would have to get the wheelchair, with my over two-hundred-pound husband, from the car to the house, and then into the house. The front door had four steps and a narrow porch; the side door directly into the kitchen had two steps and a much roomier porch. Side door seemed logical. But who builds ramps? I would need a ramp! What would it cost? Let the research begin.

Within the allotted weeks before my husband's discharge, a local church-related volunteer organization constructed a well-built, attractive ramp for just the cost of the materials. "Thank you, Lord," I sighed in gratitude. The new wheelchair arrived, so I made an appointment to learn wheelchair basics 101 at the rehabilitation center. I managed to get the chair out of its shipping carton, whereupon I practiced unfolding and folding it several times under the physical therapist's watchful eye.

"Remember to always keep your fingers out of the mechanism, and be sure you are standing sturdily and balanced," he instructed. And always—*always*—lock the wheels when someone is getting into or out of the chair. Even if the patient is sitting quietly eating, reading, or watching television, have them lock the wheels. The last thing you want is for him to move suddenly, the chair to zip out from under him, and he lands on the floor. Now, what is safety rule one?"

"*Lock the wheels!*" my husband and I both replied.

Discharge day, the staff helped me maneuver my husband into the car and then cheerily waved goodbye as we drove away. *Oh my goodness, just me and you, Babe*, I thought in a mild panic. "It will be fine," I said to my husband in a hopeful voice. He just looked tired and grim.

Home. Unload the forty-pound wheelchair. Unfold it and wheel it alongside the passenger door. Gingerly, he eased his way out of the car and then, holding onto the door frame, plunked down into the seat, sighing deeply. *Now*, I thought to myself, *slowly turn the chair and head toward the ramp*. It would not budge. Oops. "Sweetheart, please unlock your wheels. It's the two levers on the sides there, like they showed you. Thank you."

Reminder to self. Rule 2: Release brakes when desiring to move the wheelchair. We were on a roll, so to speak. Notable observation began to sink in. The walk has a slight uphill slope; the wheelchair ramp is uphill. What appeared to be a fairly slight grade was a whole 'nother thing as I pushed my two-hundred-pound-plus man up the ramp and into the house. Huff, puff, gonna develop some muscles!

Wheelchair operation was never easy. Fold, load, unfold, watch your fingers, passenger in. Push upslope, but brace back and slow the roll going downhill. Oh, so thankful for level ground! Maneuver through doors and up to tables in restaurants. Build those muscles; share these weekly outings with joy. My husband and I had wheels. Let us laugh and be glad.

Health decline in a loved one simply hurts and is not fun. Life must assume a new normal, and frustrations mount at times. And yet, I and so many other caregivers develop appreciation for conveniences such as wheelchairs that allowed for the beauty of outings to favorite or essential places. Shared experiences, even at the price of huffing and puffing and "lock your brakes" commands. Thankfulness for the kindness of strangers who would hold doors and be patient. Appreciation that in our nation, handicap ramps and access abound. Never had I appreciated how important these things were until I, myself, became a wheelchair pilot.

If we are observant, God shows us the beauty embedded in our difficult situations. While it becomes increasingly clear what we or our loved ones can no longer do, we also become sensitive to the joy of little things that build good memories and allow for as normal a life as possible. Praise our gracious God, for He remains ever with us, sustaining and giving us strength.

Beauty for Ashes

1. If you have ever been a caregiver in a difficult situation, or know someone who has, honestly recall some of the frustrating, seemingly impossible tasks that drained your/their patience and strength. How did you/they get through those moments?

2. Have you, or someone you know, ever been the one needing that special care? What were the circumstances? How did it affect you and your outlook on life? In what ways did someone come alongside you and assist? Is there any one memory that stands out as a "good moment?" What made it special?

Scripture Reflection: "To the one in despair, kindness should come from his friend" (Job 6:14).

When you are hurting, what can friends do that help you most? How can you show kindness to a friend in need?

9

Prayer Thought: "Lord, the pain of being a caregiver or receiver can be acute. In your grace, let the bad moments, the sorrows, fade from memory, and let the precious, uplifting moments shine forth. You, Father, allow life to unfold with its joys and sorrows, yet you promise you are always with us and will never leave us. Thank you. Amen."

Doctor in the House

If you lie down, you will not be afraid.

—Proverbs 3:24

When the telephone rang, interrupting my studying, I glanced at the displayed number before deciding to answer. Ah, my husband was calling from his room at the nearby nursing facility where he lived due to his declining health. I never knew quite what to expect when he called, so I whispered a quick prayer, picked up the phone, and said, "Well, hey! What's up?"

"I am so pleased," he enthused. "Thank you. I don't know how you managed it but thank you."

"Uh, you're welcome, but what is it you're so happy about?"

"My doctor!" he replied. "I have my very own doctor full-time here in my room with me. In fact, he's in the bed right next to mine. I feel so safe." He chuckled with contentment. "I feel really safe, and he is right there to talk with if I have questions. He's a really nice guy."

Interesting. I seriously had no idea what he was talking about, but given his increasing dementia, that was nothing new. Hum, I wondered what was going on down at the facility.

When I visited my husband later that afternoon, doggone it if the nurses and aids that came in the room didn't address the new, and very personable, roommate as Dr. Caldwell.

"How are you doing, Dr. Caldwell? Getting adjusted okay? Do you need anything? Just press your call button if you do," they instructed solicitously.

In visiting with my husband and his new roommate, I found Dr. Caldwell quite personable and knowledgeable most of the time, but there were those lapses indicative of, perhaps, dementia. Regardless, we all had a great time chatting and laughing. When my husband fell asleep, and I was ready to leave, I stopped by the nurse's station in the main hall out of curiosity. "My husband really likes his new roommate, and so do I. Is he really a doctor?" I asked.

"Oh, yes," the nurse on duty replied. "He was one of our facility doctors for years and years, and he has cared for many patients here. Most of us know him and respect him highly. Sadly, as you can see, his health and mental acuity have declined as he has aged, so he is now here as a resident. You'll find he has good days when his brilliance shines through, and then not-so-good days when he's pretty much shut down. We feel honored to have him in our care. Look him up online. His accomplishments are very impressive."

Indeed, they were. He was "Man of the Year" several times in our city. He established medical clinics, ran charities, was renowned for his medical research and overall brilliance. A true pioneer in various ways. How marvelous, and yet how sad, that he was my husband's new friend and roommate in a nursing care facility. Time marches on for us all.

On his good days, Dr. Caldwell and I discussed his career in medicine and my career teaching secondary English literature. He had a passion for, and broad knowledge of, Anglo-Saxon and early British culture. Given I shared his passion, on his good days we talked often about kings, queens, and literature. We both found good old Henry VIII and his wives fascinating. He was delighted to have someone who knew the subject and could keep up with him. Such fun for all of us. On his down days, he laid quietly in bed, staring at whatever was on the television, or just sleeping.

My husband continued to enjoy the doctor's company and the security of having his "very own physician right here." Then the COVID lockdowns came, visitors were barred, my husband passed on. Consequently, I have no idea if Dr. Caldwell is still living or how he is doing. I do know that even in his waning, declining days, he comforted my husband and delighted me with well-remembered conversations. He trusted in the Lord and often gave God the credit for using him in the medical field. I give God praise for using him in that nursing home to comfort my husband, the staff, and others who came his way.

God gives our lives purpose, sometimes in grand, noticeable ways, but also oftentimes in seemingly insignificant ways. I thank you, Lord, for Dr. Caldwell.

Beauty for Ashes

1. Quietly consider. What gives purpose to your life? Is purpose important?

2. God uses his people in the most unlikely places. Who blessed or influenced your life in totally unexpected ways? What did they do?

Scripture Reflection: "If you lie down, you will not be afraid" (Prov. 3:24).

Do you find this verse to be true for you? If so, in what ways does God give you such peace? If not usually true for you, what might you do to bring about this peace?

Prayer Thought: "Father, to lie down at night and quietly, fearlessly sleep is a great blessing. Help me to give all my worries and concerns to you, that I might rest, secure in your care. Amen."

Broken Heart

I want to be left alone.
I want to fall apart.
I don't need you picking up
The pieces of my broken heart.

I need my time to grieve,
To cry, to just be alone.
Is that too much to ask?

If I need you, I will find you.
If I need to talk, I'll talk.
Please just keep your distance.
Not everyone needs a crowd.

Comfort me from afar.
Let me cry alone.
Is that too much to ask?

I wish I could disappear,
Be invisible to all around.
To cry, to pray, to fix
My broken heart alone.

Is that too much to ask?
Is that too much to ask?
Is that too much to ask?

Elizabeth M. Roberts

Guard My Heart

Her children arise and call her blessed.

—Proverbs 31:28

"Uh, why is there a pistol on your dining room table?" I gingerly asked my friend, Lane, as I settled into a chair, anticipating our upcoming lunch.

"Oops. Here, let me move it," she responded, hastening to whisk it away. Lane, one of the gentlest people I know. Weird.

"Yes, well, thank you but…" I gave her a quizzical look.

"It's okay. I'm taking a course to learn how to use it safely and to get my concealed carry permit," she replied. Not quite the answer I expected.

"I know you enjoy learning new things, Lane, but this seems a tad out of character. Is there a reason?" I asked with genuine interest.

"With biological dad's history and him making threats again, I often drive home alone after dark…" she tapered off.

No more questions. Say no more. I get it. And as her dear friend, my thoughts were, *This is ridiculous. Enough.*

Lane, for years, has been a volunteer in the local Guardian ad Litem program. In our state, the Guardian ad Litem is appointed by the court to investigate and determine the needs of abused and neglected children, working alongside yet independent from the Department of Social Services. Needless to say, it can be intensely rewarding, but also heartbreaking. Always, each case demands focused time and energy, physically, mentally, and emotionally. Those volunteers who also hold down full-time jobs must negotiate with their employers about taking time off to attend court hearings and related tasks. In short, being a guardian isn't for the faint of heart.

Through the years, Lane's telephone calls tell the story.

"Please pray, friend. The court is giving the baby back to her family, to the people who neglected her older brother. We pled our case, but the judge saw it differently."

"Please pray. It's been a hectic work week, and I'll need the entire weekend to get all my investigative results worked up into a coherent report to present to the judge soon in court. I am so tired."

"Please pray. The foster parent is, and clearly has been, using the child for forced labor in her small business, not even making sure he gets to school. Please pray I can gather the facts and present a convincing case for a new placement as soon as possible."

"Please pray. One of the Social Service workers on my current case is saying untrue things about me. I am just trying to get to the truth and protect these children. It really hurts, but there's not much I can do to defend myself."

"Please pray. Biological dad is threatening all of us involved in the case... It's unnerving."

However, there are also heartwarming triumphs! The successful placement of abused youngsters in loving, caring homes, as things got sorted out, soothed their weary souls and mitigated much misery. Lane takes pride and satisfaction in knowing judges and attorneys routinely trust her conclusions, praising her carefully detailed, professional reports. And there are the children themselves.

Over time, God has granted her the reward of sometimes knowing where "her" abused and broken children have ended up, and how their lives have improved due to her efforts. Over the last several years, she has shared and kept me up to date on one of her very special young ones. A child she felt such compassion for, she looked into adopting him.

Telephone calls tell the story.

"Please pray. Kevin's relatives said some really ugly things to him while I was there. He was still crying on the back porch when I left."

"Please pray. Kevin is in a really great foster home. I'm so excited for him and the possibilities ahead."

"Please pray. My heart aches. I would love to give him the forever home he deserves, but I know the timing isn't right, and I really want to continue advocating for him."

"Please pray. I am so excited and hopeful. There is an older, childless couple who have met Kevin and are very interested in adopting him. It could be a wonderful placement."

"Please pray. Kevin has gone home with what will, Lord willing, be his new permanent mom and dad. Oh, I so hope everything works out. There's a long road ahead."

"I have a praise! I was able to do a follow up visit and go see Kevin. The family he is with couldn't be more perfect. They are wise and witty and truly understand how to be firm yet loving. God is so good."

"I have a praise! The court has finalized placement, and Kevin has his forever home."

My Guardian ad Litem friend can tell us all about lives in ashes. The most bitter, dirtiest, depressing piles of ashes ever. She stirs them up while at the same time trying to not breathe in the bitterness and hopelessness. Ashes, ashes, ashes.

And leaning on the Lord out of sheer necessity, God and she have lifted up many children from those ashes, blown the soot off them, and ultimately led them into lives of beauty they would perhaps otherwise have never known. Children like Kevin, blossoming and thriving in his forever home, bringing such joy to his adoptive parents—and to Lane. Our efforts matter. Lane's efforts matter. Together with God, we can all help bring beauty from ashes.

Beauty for Ashes

1. Volunteers are amazing people. In a society where many are driven solely by money, such folks work at often incredibly difficult tasks in order to serve and make the world a better place. Where have you, or someone you know, volunteered? What good has come out of these efforts?

2. God doesn't, strictly speaking, need us. However, he invites us to join him in serving others and improving the world. What

need(s) has possibly been laid on your heart to investigate? What are some ways you can help address this need?

Scripture Reflection: "Her children arise and call her blessed" (Prov. 31:28).

Lane has no biological children, which is the case for many people. And yet, children arise and call them blessed. Who are the children in our lives, along with perhaps our "own flesh and blood," we can touch with our caring presence? In what ways?

Prayer thought: "Father, protector, and provider, oh please be ever mindful of the children in this world. And be ever mindful of those who love them, care for them, protect them and pray for them. Sustain caregivers everywhere, for their task is not easy. In your name, amen."

Coffee and Ice Cream

For we are God's handiwork, created in Christ Jesus to do good works, which God prepared in advance for us to do.

—Ephesians 2:10

"Do you remember the time…"

"And then when the police arrived, the partyers wouldn't open the door, so the cops ticketed all their cars for parking too close to a fire hydrant, which happened to be in their front yard. Remember how the kids came running out of the house swearing and cussing, and the police just waved, laughing? It sure broke up that rowdy party!"

"And how is that new granddaughter doing, up there in DC? I know you enjoyed visiting them…"

"Welcome, new neighbors. We're all so glad you're able to join us. Let me introduce you to everyone…"

After a two-year hiatus due to COVID restrictions, the neighborhood coffee gathering, which had met for years every third Friday of every month at "Coffee Café," had resumed. When invitations were sent out for the first post-COVID restrictions meeting, we weren't sure if anyone would even come. Two stressful years was a long time. But come they did! A few the first month, more the second month, and up and running thereafter.

Coffee, ice cream, sandwiches, and smoothies plus friendly catching up and sharing of plans made for a satisfying hour or so at week's end. Strictly come as you are, pull up a chair, and "How's things going?"

Connie, an older widow who had been pretty isolated, sighed contentedly. "You know, this neighborhood meeting is just so special. I love my neighbors, and I love living here."

It had not always been this way. In fact, previous to the eight or more years we had been meeting, things were quite different. In those days, everyone up and down the street basically got along, mainly because we hardly knew each other. You know, the usual keep-to-one's-self suburban neighborhood. Folks knew I taught at the local high school. Neighbor Larry, who was retired, faithfully plowed the street and our driveways with his yard tractor if we had one of our rare Southern snowstorms. Mindy had a beagle and kept her yard nice. Susan was a nurse, and her husband loved horticulture. They had a nice compact greenhouse. Connie had cared for her husband until he passed on then stayed mostly to herself. As we all did, actually.

Oh, we'd wave from our porch at someone walking down the street, and maybe even chat in the mornings getting in our cars to head to work. Most people knew which dog or cat lived where. I had lived there for twenty some years, knew most names, and life seemed normal. When one of the "kids" got married, some of us went to the weddings and such. But otherwise, there was not much socializing. I never gave it much thought.

And then Anne and her husband moved in across the street. Her two dogs, a beagle, and a beagle-basset mix, frequently let everyone know of their presence in the early evening with their melodious baying. My dogs, across the street, loved to bark at them from my fenced backyard, and we would enjoy listening to the hounds yodeling back, waving to each other from our front patios over coffee.

One day, the phone rang. "Hi! This is Anne, across the street? I was just wondering if you might like to join me for coffee and pastries some morning, just to get better acquainted."

"Sounds great," I replied to this welcome, if unexpected, invitation. We set a day, time, and place.

She wasn't there. I waited and waited at Boros Road Coffee Shop and finally gave her a call. "Hey, I'm here at Boros. Did I miss you somehow?"

"Oh! I'm here at Corner Coffee Café. That's where I'd suggested," she replied.

"Oops! My bad. I'm just so used to going to Boros, I simply forgot you'd said Corner Coffee." Well, I was off to a great start here!

"It's okay. Just come on over. I'll wait for you," she graciously replied.

In no time, we were laughing together at my memorable "first impression" over steaming mugs of coffee and yummy muffins.

"Let's do this once a month," Anne suggested. "It's been fun. If we set a firm day, we can plan for it and not just let it fade away."

"Good idea, "I agreed, "and perhaps we could invite a few others in the neighborhood to join us."

"Sure, why not!"

And so, an almost ten-year tradition began. Neighbors came, including, after several months, some of the men. Meeting monthly, the Neighborhood Gatherings at Corner Coffee Café is still going strong, bringing people together.

Not long ago, I asked Anne why she made that first phone call to me. "Well, we'd moved in not that long ago, and I didn't have family around other than my husband. Kinda lonely and all. You liked dogs. I liked dogs. You seemed the logical person to reach out to. Plus, my church was strongly urging us to get involved with other people, share our faith, strive to be encouragers and where better to start than right in my neighborhood? Frankly, I never thought it would grow like it did and keep on going as it has. We've shared good times and bad, witnessed to each other about God's love, and done life together. God certainly can use us to bring about the most unexpected things, can't he? Makes me feel very humble."

"Yes, he can," I thought. "Yes, he can."

Beauty from Ashes

1. Ponder a time when you, or someone else, worked up the courage to reach out and connect with another person, not knowing how it might be received. What was the outcome?

2. It is interesting how traditions can get started. What is a family, neighborhood, or other tradition you enjoy? What were its origins? If you don't know, perhaps it would be interesting to find out.

Scripture Reflection: "For we are God's handiwork, created in Christ Jesus to do good works, which God prepared in advance for us to do" (Eph. 2:10).

What are some of the good works God has let you perform for his service and glory?

Prayer Thought: "Father, thank you for loving us and letting us perform works you have prepared, that we might bless others and bring glory to you. Let us be ever sensitive to the Spirit's promoting in our lives, that we use every opportunity to do your will. Amen."

Chalk It Up

Watch out! Be on guard against all kinds of greed; life
does not consist in an abundance of possessions.

—Luke 12:15

The beginning of my life of crime stands out clearly in my memory. That moment when I stepped from doing wrongs in childish innocence to coveting, planning, and executing a heist. I was nine years old and in Mrs. Hersher's fourth grade class. I absolutely liked and respected her, but then again…

It was partly her fault. Doesn't the Bible say, "Lead us not into temptation"? She did that; she tempted me. I was only nine years old, just a kid. She should have known better than to lure me into a carefully plotted purloining. And she shared the blame with my father, of all people.

Actually, it was Dad who was mostly responsible. After all, I was only nine years old and just a kid. Did I even know right from wrong? Well, okay. Obviously, I did know my upcoming criminal action was wrong, or I would not have stealthily planned it.

Dad found out I loved using white and yellow chalk to draw pictures on the sidewalk. "Hey, you know what?" he enthused. "They sell blackboard paint at the hardware store. If I cut a nice piece of plywood, paint it, and attach it to the basement wall in the laundry room, you could draw while Mom does the laundry. What do you think?"

"Yes! Let's do it, Dad! I'd love my very own blackboard."

The blackboard turned out great. Dad equipped it with a new blackboard eraser, a box of white chalk, and a soft rag to wash it with as needed. I used that soft rag frequently as I happily spent hours drawing or doing arithmetic homework problems. Much more fun than paper and pencil! Gratitude filled my childlike heart.

Until that fateful day. Mrs. Hersher wrote five arithmetic problems at the side of the long classroom blackboard. One by one, she called a student up to demonstrate how to solve a problem, handing him or her a piece of *colored chalk*. A red one, or a blue one, or a green one, or a violet one. No white. No yellow. Colors!

My pulse picked up. I could not wait until it was my turn. The chalk was lovely. And there were more unopened, brand-new boxes stacked on the classroom table by the door. Each box filled with six lovely colors. Oh, the beautiful pictures I could draw. I want, I must have, I deserve a box of that colored chalk. Mrs. Hersher has lots of boxes; she will never even miss one.

How to go about this. Let me see. I was a walker student, meaning that since I lived close, I did not take a school bus. Now, Mrs. Hersher went out directly after class to supervise bus loading, so if I managed to stay after school just a few minutes, I could pull it off. The dismissal bell finally rang.

"Mrs. Hersher," I said, "I'm not quite done with my work here. Can I stay behind just a few minutes and finish?"

"Sure, Sandy. That's fine. I've got to go supervise the buses. Bye."

She left. I packed up my backpack and, after a quick glance around, strolled by the table and deftly snatched a precious box. Success was mine! I was officially a thief.

Have you ever noticed how one sin seems to lead to another? "Now that's really pretty," my mom noted when she came to the basement to run some clothes. "Green grass. Blue sky. Pretty flowers. Very nice. I'm surprised your father got you colored chalk, seeing it's more expensive. That was nice of him."

"Uh," I stuttered, caught off guard. "A friend gave it to me."

"Well, how nice. Did you thank her?"

"Yes, Mom. I did." A thief and now a liar.

And that was that. Did I return the chalk out of guilt? No. Did I even really give it a second thought? No. Did I enjoy my ill-gotten gain? Yes, extremely so. We are talking hardened nine-year-old master thief here. Mrs. Hersher never mentioned missing a box. I doubt she even noticed.

However, the intriguing thing is decades later I still remember the incident, and I have right along over the past years. My "innocence" ended at nine years old and accountability—awareness—began. Since the event, I have asked forgiveness for that and many other transgressions, as I have grown in the Lord. From the ashes of that lost innocence has come increasing awareness of how precious and beautiful Jesus's sacrifice was for us. How frail we humans are, with our innate inclination to sin. And yet, from that awareness comes the beauty and joy of being forgiven and restored. Appreciation and gratitude spring forth anew.

Beauty from Ashes

1. Do you remember your first deliberate sin or transgression? What was it? Why did you do it? How did it turn out?

2. How has this incident affected you, assuming it has? Ponder the miracle of forgiveness, as we are so prone to transgress.

Scripture Reflection: "Watch out! Be on guard against all kinds of greed; life does not consist in an abundance of possessions" (Luke 12:15).

How is this verse speaking specifically to *you*? What do you seem to constantly need to guard against? How do you view possessions?

Prayer thought: "Father, forgive me my sinful ways. I am so skilled at blaming others and justifying myself, but in my heart, I know how prone I am to sin. Father, I confess my sins this day to you and ask your forgiveness. Amen."

You Surround Me

You surround me in your beauty,
You surround me in your love.
You surround me in your comfort.
For I am yours alone.

Your love is above all others.
No one can rise above.
For you alone are mighty.
For you alone I love.

Elizabeth M. Roberts

Birds, Not Bombs

I know every bird on the mountains.

—Psalm 50:11

Whenever an airplane flew over, ChaSa would stop whatever he was doing in the garden and stare intently at the sky. When helicopters passed by at a fairly low altitude, he would invariably drop his gardening tool and run into the stand of nearby evergreen trees. After it passed, he would hesitantly come out of the copse, watching the sky intently, and get back to work.

On occasions when I'd be working at the kitchen sink, able to observe him from the window, I wondered what terrors, what memories were racing through his mind. Given he spoke very little English, and I spoke only a few Hmong words he had taught me—his native tongue in Laos—we couldn't discuss it. I doubt he would have wanted to share the nightmares with me, even if he could.

When, in the early 1970s, the communists overran Laos in Southeast Asia, a local church-related refugee resettlement organization asked for volunteers to help in various ways with a family of six being sent to our area. A father, mother, ChaSa's mother-in-law and three elementary-school-age children. A rental house or apartment, clothes, household items, school supplies, and work opportunities were solicited. A goal was to get ChaSa, the father, employed full or part time so he could have the dignity of helping to support his family.

"It's very important," the agency people instructed, "that the refugees be involved in the community in productive ways. These are very proud, intelligent, hardworking people who cooperated with the United States during the war and have had to flee for their lives.

Agrarian work would be especially helpful, as it is something this family is familiar with. Being out and about will also help them make friends and learn some English."

Upon talking it over, my husband and I decided we had the room out back for a large vegetable garden, even though we had never had one before. We had the space, and the hopefully resulting produce could be given away to ChaSa's family and to the agency, who could share it with others. Plus, it would provide employment for ChaSa several days a week from spring to fall. We hired him.

ChaSa and his family lived in our small town, about a mile or so from our home, which was somewhat "out in the country." For him, walking to and from the job was no problem, he told us through the interpreter, as he daily walked much further in his native land.

The early days were interesting, especially when he was introduced to our large, lovable, black standard poodle. When Danielle happily wiggled all over, greeting him eagerly to make friends, ChaSa started laughing in absolute delight. He patted her big poofy topknot, tweaked her tasseled ears, patted her curly body, and lightly batted her pom-pomed tail as she wagged it excitedly back and forth. She adored this open-hearted, unpretentious man, and from that moment on, she became his "gardening partner." I don't think ChaSa had seen any big poodles in Laos!

Starting a garden from scratch in untouched soil was no easy task. We had it roto-tilled to break up the dirt in preparation, but ChaSa put in many hours patiently working with hoe and rake, breaking clods of earth into a suitable texture for planting. Once, at a team meeting, I expressed through the interpreter that I hoped ChaSa wasn't hopelessly bored. "Oh no!" ChaSa avowed. "This is what I know. This is what farmers do. We patiently prepare the soil day by day. Why would I be bored? I listen to the quiet, to the birds. You have many birds with sweet songs I'm not familiar with, so I am learning about them. I watch the cars going up and down the road, and I enjoy being with silly Danielle. And even the airplanes I grow used to. Never does a bomb fall or gunfire sound. No, I am not bored, but at peace. Thank you for letting me work."

What the family's previous life was like, when every airplane or helicopter possibly carried death and destruction, I can't fathom. When falling bombs literally reduced villages and fields to ashes remains beyond my understanding.

As the months went by, the garden produced amazing quantities of corn, tomatoes, beans, squash, and other nutritious vegetables. There was plenty for us, with an abundance for ChaSa to take home to his family and share with other refugee friends. His pride at growing and sharing all this bounty, produced by his work and God's goodness, healed many wounds and obviously gave him purpose and pleasure. Beauty, beauty, beauty everywhere. His family was safe from the ravages of war. Tall corn, swaying trees, and hosts of opportunistic birds (ChaSa eventually built a delightful scarecrow) filled his life with joy.

Come late fall, after the harvest, ChaSa and his family, along with several others in the area, were resettled in another state, which already had a thriving Hmong/Laotian community and culture. Several of his relatives were already there, so of course ChaSa and his family were eager to go to them. We were happy for them, but their departure left a real void in our lives. They had taught us much and enriched our lives immeasurably.

Come spring, we leveled the garden area and reseeded it with grass, returning it to the lawn it originally had been. The garden had served its purpose, growing vegetables and nourishing the lives and souls of God's precious people, especially giving ChaSa beauty instead of ashes.

Beauty for Ashes

1. If you have been so fortunate as to befriend / help someone in truly dire straits, reflect on the experience. How did you help them? How, in turn, did they benefit, bless, and help you?

2. The Bible makes it clear we are to welcome the stranger, offer hospitality, care about the friendless, needy, lonely, and lost. What are some ways you do this? Why do you think God wants us to be mindful of those less fortunate than we?

Scripture Reflection: "I know every bird on the mountains" (Ps. 50:11).

ChaSa found solace in watching and listening to the birds as he worked his field. What do you find peace and solace in? Why?

Prayer Thought: "Father, keep us mindful that you love all of your children and care about them. Soften our hearts and keep us mindful of the needs of others, especially their need to know you. Let us be a light in the world, pointing people to you through our actions. Amen."

I'll Fly Away

How the mighty have fallen.

—2 Samuel 1:25

Ponies are the chihuahuas of the equine world. Now, this is not necessarily a negative statement, just an honest one. Fact is, both ponies and chihuahuas tend to prefer their own kind, adore and trust only their owners, and ain't got no time for strangers. (Pony and chihuahua owners, you know in your hearts this is true.)

"Buttons was a Shetland pony," recounts my sister Beth. "She was my best friend for the time I had her. I was eight years old when she came. I was the main person who cared for her, and she trusted me. In fact, I was the only person she tolerated riding her. I could jump on bareback or with the saddle, and then ride like the wind with no problems. It was a mutual love that we had for each other.

"I spent hours riding, walking, brushing, and just talking to her. As young as I was, she let me do everything with no problems. I fully trusted her, and she trusted me. Cleaning her barn area was my job, and I didn't mind it at all. Thinking about her just warms my heart, as if it were yesterday. I loved her so much."

Buttons came to my father's pasture free of charge to be a companion for my father's full-size horse. Dappled gray, big soulful eyes, and—you guessed it—cute as a button. Her owners wanted a loving home for her, and my father thought his youngest daughter would enjoy having a pony all her own. A match made in heaven.

And then big sister, me, came home for a visit to the family, having moved to another state several years ago. The know-it-all big sister, nice but bossy. You know, a big sister. And an experienced horse person who took pride in her ability to ride.

"Well, hey, Beth! She is absolutely adorable and looks fabulous," I enthused. "Let's see you ride her. Dad tells me you are really good."

"Okay," Beth agreed, all smiles. "Let me show you. I have to brush her good first to get all the loose hair off, 'cause I ride mostly bareback. I just hop on and off we go."

As she talked, her small hands energetically curried up the dust on Button's coat, and then flicked it away until her little body gleamed. Next, Beth picked and cleaned each little hoof. Finally, she slipped the bridle over Button's head and the bit into her mouth.

"There," she said proudly, as I looked on with admiration. "All set. Now watch me."

With young kid pride, she jumped up and draped herself over Button's back then swung her leg over and sat up proudly. Picking up the reins, she made a quiet clicking sound to the little mare, and off they went around the backyard, racing the wind. Trot, trot, trot. Lope, lope, lope. Lovely circles, starts and stops. Finally, she rode back over to me, so happy.

"Isn't she just the best! I love her," Beth enthused, somewhat out of breath.

"Hey, could I ride her?" I asked, thinking how fun it had looked.

Looking aghast, my little sis shook her head. "No. She only lets me ride her. And you are too big anyway."

Well, there was that, but hey, just a stroll in the yard can't hurt. "Oh, come on," I said, chuckling. "Just once around, and we'll just walk."

As Beth shook her head no, I eased past her. "Hey there, cutie," I said to Buttons, stroking her face gently. "Can I take a ride?" She pretty much ignored me, standing quietly and looking straight ahead.

"What a good girl you are!" Giving her a pat, I draped myself over her back, swung my leg over, and off I went! Literally. As in, the amazing flying would-be pony rider. Airborne, know-it-all big sister up, up, and away.

"I'll fly away, oh lordy, I'll fly away..." briefly flitted through my mind, the gospel song memory ending when the inevitable landing took place. "Oaf," I gasped, the breath knocked out of me. Then

I lay quietly, assessing for any damage as my riding instructors had taught me.

"Are you okay?" Beth cried out, racing over. Buttons also moseyed over and nudged me with her nose. I swear I could hear her chuckling as she viewed her handiwork.

"Yeah, I'm fine," I said. What was that Bible verse? Pride goes before the flying fall?

Once she knew I was okay, my little twerpy sister hugged her pony and laughed. "That was an amazing sight! You went up in the air. I *told* you she only lets me ride her!" And then she led Buttons through the pasture gate and turned her lose. "I love my pony," she assured me. Nodding, I limped beside her back to the house.

Humiliation. Pain. Know-it-all pride. Trampling on a young person's feelings. Ashes of regret at thoughtlessness. And finally, the anti-climactic comedown. Therein lay the blessing, the beauty. A true lesson in the importance of humility and respect for others, animals and humans. Sometimes, puffed up fools need a painful lesson in wisdom.

Beauty From Ashes

1. Have you a memory of being unkind, bossy, know-it-all prideful toward someone? In what ways were you thoughtless and overconfident?

2. So how did your pride "go before the fall"? What taught you a valuable lesson and painfully increased your wisdom?

Scripture Reflection: "How the mighty have fallen" (2 Samuel 1:25).

Look up the context of this verse in 2 Samuel chapter 1. What were the circumstances that prompted this thought?

Prayer thought: "Father, how easy it is to feel superior, to ignore someone's feelings, to be prideful. Forgive me, Lord, when I have acted arrogantly and help me always, humbly, remember every gift and talent I have, comes from you. Amen."

Well, Well, Well

We know that all things work together for
good to those who love God.

—Romans 8:28

The craziest, work-long hours, most exhausting time for a dog-grooming business is, hands down, the Thanksgiving/Christmas holiday season, and my shop was hectic. The phone would not stop ringing as people scrambled to book their dogs for a spruce-up. My employees and I labored hard to work everyone in while still maintaining our high-quality standards. Fortunately, only a few days before Christmas, all was well. Long tiring hours but satisfied customers. And then, well, things were not well.

"There's no water," my dog bather informed. "I can't bathe this poodle."

"What?" I asked, only half paying attention.

"There's no water," she patiently repeated.

If there is one thing crucial for grooming a dog, it is water. Without water, a dirty dog remains a dirty dog. A groomer can rough clip a dirty dog, but it is impossible to scissor or properly finish the cut unless the animal is squeaky clean. Nothing to be done but call the owner, send the dog home with assurances we would rebook as soon as possible, and be thankful it was the last client of the day. After we cleaned up the shop and closed, I got on the phone and called the well technician who had originally set up my well and installed the well pump. (No, no city water lines out here in the country!)

"Hey, Mr. Laird," I said when he answered. As calmly as possible, I explained the situation. "Can you come take a look at it as soon as possible? I know you're probably busy."

He chuckled. "I'll be there first thing tomorrow morning."

"I'm impressed you will come that soon. Thank you."

"You're welcome, but given it's been in the twenties or so for a few weeks here, and right before Christmas, not many folks are putting in wells, let me assure you. It's my slow period."

Well, yeah. That made sense. One person's drop-dead rush season is another's quiet spell.

Eight in the morning, and his Laird the Well Man bright blue truck pulled into the driveway beside the manhole that housed the well pump. Dawn was barely breaking, and it was cold. An occasional Arctic gust swept down from the Pennsylvania hills, chilling things even more. From a window, I cozily watched as he removed the manhole cover and headed down the steps. At least he would be out of the wind while he worked! Shortly, his head reappeared as he climbed out, went to his truck, and turned on his wench. Pulling a cable behind him, down he went again. Moments later, he came up again, carefully working the wench and watching his lines. Slowly the worn-out well pump rose from the manhole, to be laid aside.

A brand near pump was attached to the line and let down into the depths, followed by Mr. Laird. In no time, he was up and tapping at the door. "Check and be sure your water's running," he requested. It was!

"Pump was burned out. I put that in quite a while back, if you recall, so you got your money's worth out of that pump! Kinda bad timing for you, though."

"I can't begin to tell you how much I appreciate your coming," I said. "What do I owe you?"

"Give me a minute." He sat down at the table and computed parts, labor, emergency rush fee, and filled out the form.

Ouch, I thought. Worth every penny, but still, ouch. Oh well. There was no other option, and at least I was back in business. After I wrote out the check, I offered him a cup of hot coffee and some doughnuts.

"Mr. Laird," I said. "I've noticed the entire time you've been here, you've been very cheerful, even when you were out there working in the cold. You were humming as you figured my bill, and you seem happy now. If I had to work with a well, getting wet, in this horrible weather, no way I'd be cheerful! Especially for someone wanting a rush job. I'd be a grumpy camper, for sure. I truly admire you."

Finishing his coffee, he set the mug down and looked me in the eye. "Ms. Still, I know this was an awkward thing for you, and I'm glad I could help. But let me share something. For me, it was God's answer to prayer. Work's been slow, and my three little kids were getting no Christmas. With Christmas just a few days away, you know what I'm going to do on my way home? I'm going by the tree lot down the road and getting a Christmas tree for my young'uns. My kids and wife will go crazy when I drive in with a tree on the truck roof. This job is giving my family a real celebration, and that's the truth. Honestly, I never even noticed the cold."

When he left, I sat at the table humbled, a song in my heart. Yes, I was inconvenienced, and yes, I had to spend some money. But God chose me to bless Mr. Laird and his family. To give them joy and a celebration of Jesus's birth. Sighing deeply, I picked up the telephone and began to rebook my clients, working them in before the holiday somehow, somewhere, even if it meant overtime hours. "All will be well," I whispered. And it was.

Beauty for Ashes

1. Even though this happened years ago, I still feel the emotion of being used to bless someone else. Can you recall a time when God clearly used you to aid or encourage another? What took place? How did you react?

2. Being used of God usually costs us in some fashion. Inconvenience, money, heartache, suffering oftentimes. What did the event in question one cost you? Despite the cost, would you do it again? Why or why not?

Scripture Reflection: "We know that all things work together for good to those who love God" (Rom. 8:28).

Do you believe this is the case? Do you have doubts? Obviously, all things are *not* good, so what does this scripture actually mean?

Prayer thought: "Lord, you have called us to follow you, no matter the cost. Give me the wisdom to see your leading in life's situations. Grow my faith, that I can trust all things will work together for good and your glory. I am humbled and honored that you even consider using me. Amen."

"Go Away, God"

Wait for the Lord; be strong and take heart and wait for the Lord.
—Psalm 27:14

"No, Lord. Just take the desire out of my heart and leave me be," I thought yet again. "Go away, God."

Uproot my life? Venture into the unknown? Take on seemingly endless challenges? Uh, not very appealing.

"Lord, I'd like to point out I don't even have my own car, and my husband drives our family car to work. So no way I can get to classes at the university, forty minutes away, to take courses at all hours. Given there are no buses or carpools, this is just impossible."

Despite my pleas, the dream, the calling, of becoming a high school English teacher just would not leave my heart. In fact, over the last decade, it had only continued to grow.

"Father, my home business is highly successful, but keeping it going while trying to attend classes, not to mention studying, for several years seems—overwhelmingly exhausting, practically impossible. And once my student teaching semester comes, I would have to pretty much close the business down. Bye, bye income. Hello loans and debt."

Serving at our church as a youth group leader for the high school students had only fanned the flames of my desire to teach. It was obvious I related very well with young people, and they related well to me. I loved designing lessons and activities for them, and they enjoyed my leadership.

"Father, you do know I'm thirty years old now, and I've not been in formal classes for a good while. And I never was good at math, so this many years away from my last high school math course—not good. As I've expressed to you before, Lord, this whole idea really doesn't make any sense."

No, it made no sense. It was impossible. Upon reflection, reluctantly, I decided it would not hurt to drive up to the university campus come Saturday, when I could take the car, and just look around. See how long the drive would take. Walk the halls, if any buildings were open. Talk to students who might be around. That sort of thing. Just scope it out. Why not?

So I did. I strolled around various buildings, soaking up the ambience of the science hall, the gymnasiums, the horticultural gardens, envisioning myself there as a student. The dream was beginning to become more real, more concrete, more obtainable, as I realized how welcome and comfortable I felt on the campus. Before heading home, I sat quietly on a bench under a tree, facing the main building with its classic brick walls, bell tower, and Grecian columns. Peace filled my soul as I talked to God.

"Father, I feel wrapped in welcome here, filled with hope and excitement. If it is your will, even though I have no idea how it can be achieved, I will launch out in faith and apply for admission for next semester. If I am not accepted, well, that will solve the issue. However, if accepted, I will humbly begin the journey of becoming a high school teacher, as I believe you want me to be. You, Father, will surely have to open doors, for I see no pathway at all for success in this. Amen."

Clouds drifted across blue sky. Sunlight warmed my shoulders. And in my heart, mind, and soul a definite mind shift took place. The decision became finalized. I would take the necessary steps to become a university student. Rising, I went into the main building and took a university catalog of admission procedures, protocols, and class offerings from a rack in the hall. There was so very much I needed to learn and figure out. Time to head home and start reading. Time to talk to my husband, for this would very much affect him. Time to begin turning my life upside down. Time to trust the Lord as I began slowly destroying my current, comfortable life, leaving it behind and embracing the scary future which God had persistently laid on my heart.

"Father, going back to school and becoming a teacher was, indeed, probably the hardest venture I have ever taken. Business gone. Debt. Recession in the area I was living leading to three layoffs in three years of teaching (last hired—first fired) necessitating a move to another state to find employment. Learning my job. Long commutes. And yet—thank you, Lord."

Looking back, I do not know how I survived it all, but do you know what? I did. Others did and do. Following what the Lord lays on our hearts to pursue for his glory and the benefit of others often is difficult. When Jesus said, "Take up your cross," he was not kidding in most cases.

But there it is again, that great truth. The Lord "bestows on them a crown of beauty, instead of ashes." He promised he would, and he keeps every promise.

Beauty for Ashes

1. In my case, patiently abiding in God's promise led ultimately to a successful career influencing many teenagers throughout the years. Often, though, following God's way leads to seemingly less successful results. Have you experienced, or do you know someone who has experienced, a venture for the Lord that appeared to not end well? What happened? Ultimately, did a positive result emerge from the circumstance? Explain.

2. Some people claim following Jesus guarantees "health and wealth." How might you respond to them? What biblical basis do you have for your response? What life experiences?

Scripture Reflection: "Wait for the Lord; be strong and take heart and wait for the Lord" (Ps. 27:14).

What in this verse touches your heart and mind? What does it mean to wait for the Lord? What does it mean to be strong and take heart?

Prayer Thought: "Lord, oh my goodness, yielding to you and following what appears to be your will can be so scary, so difficult, that it can just overwhelm. Father, give me the patience and trust to just take the first step, knowing that you will open doors according to your will. We thank you, Lord, for even considering using us for your kingdom and glory. Amen."

Roots and Runners

Let your roots grow down into him, and
let your life be built on him.

—Colossians 2:7

"Plant wisteria," the garden center adviser suggested wistfully. "It's so lovely! Or perhaps ornamental bamboo would work well in that spot."

"Uh, don't those plants tend to take over?" the dubious shopper inquired.

The garden center employee shrugged. "Well, of course, they have that potential, but if you plant them in a confined area, they can be easily controlled."

I believe that was confidently said about kudzu, that plant from the orient that arrived in 1876 to serve as a quick growing (as in a foot a day) ground cover and forage plant. Gallantly, kudzu has marched forth, climbing to the tops of tall trees, up and across overhead power lines, engulfing barns, houses and—it is surreptitiously said—more than one soundly sleeping cow.

No one, as far as I know, would ever suggest kudzu for a yard, but wisteria? Bamboo? They have and do.

I have been battling wisteria gone wild in the yard of a house I purchased not long ago. Wisteria roots and runners have spread out everywhere and require a constant vigil of pulling, cutting, digging out, and nuking, when possible, with herbicide. Here is the thing with wisteria runners. A delicate little leafy shoot springs up, waving in the breeze. I go to pull it up. It is attached, very attached, to a long in-the-ground rope like runner. Two to three feet of pulled up runner later, I usually concede defeat, go to the shed, and get the pruning shears. Major surgery is required, as the runner is too tough to break manually. Then on to the next "delicate little leafy shoot." It requires a constant and persistent vigil. Progress has been made, and I have hope of winning this battle. My friend who purchased a property with ornamental bamboo I am not so sure about.

Barbara versus the Bamboo remains an ongoing saga. She and the family hack, chop and rip it out. Thinking it was gone, they went away for a short vacation. Upon return, a sea of bamboo shoots had also returned. Getting desperate, they hired a small bulldozer to come in and literally dig down and scrape away the roots. Ah, that seemed to do it, for a brief time. And then…new bamboo shoots everywhere. Reluctantly, the next step was powerful herbicides. Seemingly, bamboo absolutely loves powerful herbicides. Last I heard, Barbara and family were talking dynamite.

Both the wisteria and the ornamental bamboo can, indeed, be lovely. (The kudzu, not so much.) Both can serve a decorative purpose when properly contained and controlled. The problem is, they spread their roots quietly, silently, persistently underground, gaining more territory each growing season. Until, one day, it dawns on the property owner that the bamboo patch has spread considerably. That the wisteria has wrapped itself around the oak tree almost to the top and is choking the life out of it. Let the battle to contain and eradicate begin!

Sin in our lives works much like invasive plants. How we love to believe that we can control every questionable activity or habit! And often, like a property owner, it appears we can. Our lives look rather good overall, no problem. No evidence of silent, unnoticeable, creeping tendrils or shoots of looming takeover and destruction.

"I've got this. Everything is fine. It's under control," we can rationalize. Until the time comes when we no longer have everything under control. The evidence of our failure, the shoots, and runners, have become all too evident. At that point, we can either give up in despair, or we can begin the hard work of ripping sin up by the roots, persistently and consistently. And it can be a battle royal, fighting habits and behaviors we long for and used to love. Issues that are now destroying our lives.

We need, we long for, the wisdom and help of our Master Gardener, Jesus. The One who designed and planted the first garden,

Eden. The one who constantly warns us, "Don't plant the kudzu of sin. Beware of thinking you can control everything." The One who urges us to let our roots grow down into Him.

Fortunately, the Lord forgives us our foolishness if we acknowledge our mistakes, and then set about uprooting, blasting out and killing the invasive sin in our lives, with His assistance. May we be deeply rooted in Him, in His word, sending out beneficial and worthwhile runners that tell others of God's goodness and blessing.

Beauty for Ashes

1. Recall a time in life when you battled nature, be it a determined to die potted plant or an out-of-control, overgrown plant. What steps did you take to prevail? Did you succeed?

2. Has there ever been an "I can easily control this" habit or sin in your life, which you ended up having to battle? If so, how did it get started? Have you prevailed and won, or is it an ongoing struggle?

Scripture Refection: "Let your roots grow down into him, and let your life be built on him" (Col. 2:7).

Explain some ways you nurture your growth in the Lord, that you may develop strong roots in faith.

Prayer Thought: "Father, I pray for the wisdom to recognize seemingly innocent things in my life which could end up engulfing me in sin. Help me, also, to trust you to help me subdue and escape from anything that currently displeases you. Lord, I ask for mercy in your name, amen."

Of Squirrels and Vultures

There is a path no fowl knows, and which
the vulture's eye has not seen.

—Job 28:7

What a gorgeous early spring morning it was. One of those days that make you glad to be alive, with perfect humidity and temperature as the sun peeked over the treetops, brightening the eastern sky. Cardinals flitted from fence post to fence post. Wrens twittered busily in the bushes. A distant dog barked. My little Dandie Dinmont terrier, Calvin, barked in reply, then joyfully rolled in the dewy grass.

I slowly and deliberately strolled about the yard, working my way along my neighbor's fence line, looking for invasive English ivy to pull out by the roots. I was determined to eradicate the out-of-control menace from my recently purchased property. It was such a blessing to have this cool, shady, lovely day. The ever-present squirrels ran about the yard, digging, chattering, and eyeing each other. My neighbor's towering water oaks supplied the little creatures with a bounty of acorns. Cal lay quietly in the grass watching them, a contented look on his obviously happy face. The numerous squirrels and he had decided to coexist quite a ways back.

Ah, squirrels. Leaping and chasing and…hanging by the neck from an ivy enwrapped tree limb, way up there, dead? *Oh no*, I thought. *How sad.* Yes, it was definitely dangling by the neck, its little feet motionless in the morning air. The pathetic creature swayed from its gallows as a passing breeze swept the tree's branches. I could clearly see it had a loop of dead English ivy vine around its neck. The little guy must have put his head through the vine to get an acorn, and then could not get untangled. "Hey, little one," I sighed. "I hope you died quickly, without suffering terror or pain."

As I pondered the scene, it struck me that, given the squirrel was way higher than I could possibly reach, I would have to endure him slowly decaying until he fell to Earth. Depressed, I walked away and plopped down in a lawn chair. There was nothing to be done, so I sat quietly; the glow had faded from a perfect morning. Cal lay at my feet as I opened the book I was currently reading and settled in. Peace reigned.

Until, out of the corner of my eye, a swooping black shape went by. Then another. I slowly raised my eyes only to see a truly macabre sight. Quietly, eerily, five large turkey vultures had lined themselves up on the ridge of my neighbor's roof. The rising sun shone on them like a spotlight. Several of the black birds shook themselves and then slowly extended their wings as they perched. Side by side, wings touching, it truly was a scene from some horror movie.

The vultures watched me. I watched them. Calvin lifted his head, looked at the birds, and then quietly went around behind my chair, peeking out. While the vultures looked threatening, I knew they were not going to attack, but why were they assembling?

Without warning, the largest one suddenly and silently left the ridge, swooped straight for the ivy-covered tree, and faster than I could follow, the hanging squirrel was gone. Quickly the other four birds followed, and the congregation disappeared up into the fluffy white clouds. Gone, just like that. A dramatic and stunning reminder of God's provision for his creatures. The cycle of death and life, enacted before my eyes. That unfortunate squirrel's untimely end would provide life-giving nourishment to the vultures. Its death was not in vain.

The sun rose higher. Cal ventured forth from behind my chair and started nosing happily about the yard. I closed my book, relieved that I would not have to observe a slowly decaying squirrel day after day and headed into the house. Good came from the sad; God's creatures had fulfilled their created purposes.

Beauty for Ashes

1. The cycle of life. Ponder an incident in your life when you became acutely aware of how birth, life and death can complete God's purposes.

2. Each of us has a unique gift and function in life. Select one function in life you believe God has given you to uniquely fulfill. How have you carried out your assignment?

Scripture Reflection: "There is a path no fowl knows, and which the vulture's eye has not seen" (Job 28:7).

As you journey with God, what is your path currently like? How would you describe it? Is it taking you away from or toward God? How?

Prayer Thought: "Lord, Father, we praise you that out of death, life can spring. That for your children, while our ashes may be 'in the closet,' our spirits live eternally with you. Amen."

The Heart Is Full of Grief

The heart is full of grief; it sears the soul.
Talk not to me of hopes that lie ahead.
The loneliness alone doth take its toll.
In truth, at times, I so envy the dead.

I'll take a trip and leave this gloom behind!
My friends I'll see, so we can gladly roam.
The dog and I stroll paths, a peace we find.
Yet then, oh, once again I must come home.

"Oh, death, where is your sting?" It's in my heart.
Sickness and death and fear are all around.
Dear Lord, most high, will you not take our part?
Then in the storm I hear that quiet sound:

"I give beauty for ashes, do not fear."
In peace I rest; I know my God is near.

Day Is Done

Precious in the sight of the Lord is the death of His saints.

—Psalm 116:15

He dropped on one knee and held out the folded flag to my younger sister. Beth tenderly took it, tears trickling down her face.

"In honor of his service," the military officer said, as he arose, saluted her, and returned to his place in the armed guard standing at attention at my father's funeral.

The rifle salute was over. The haunting notes of Taps, played on the trumpet, had floated away on the morning air. Friends and family sat or stood in respectful silence, reflecting on a life well lived. How many times, especially as Dad got older, had we listened quietly to the same army stories, told over and over with joy at the memories. The story of how he and our mother met. Of how she followed him to the army bases during World War II, where he served as a medical assistant, and she worked as an office secretary. Each time he retold those precious memories, his face lit up, and his laughter rang out once again. Time didn't exist, and he was a young man back in the late 1940s, rebuilding the world after the ravages of war. Starting a family. Facing a brave new world full of hope and promise. Plying his trade as a master carpenter and skilled roofer.

Given his satisfaction with a career as a roofer, he lived much of his life on the heights. Barns. Churches. Commercial buildings. Ostentatious multistoried houses. Oh my goodness, the work was often grueling. It was cold in winter, if the weather even permitted the crews to roof. Summer brought blistering heat under the relentless sun, though the men would head out early in the predawn to get a cooler start.

My father wasn't a big man, but he was strong. Roofers had to be, back then, in order to sling a bundle of shingles over their shoulder and climb up a ladder. There were no hydraulic high lifts back in the day to deposit the heavy bundles on the roof. The bane of his career was ever watchful housewives. He regaled us often at dinner with tales of fussy homeowners, usually mimicking their voices.

"Now don't you step on my pansies!" a lady would fuss. "You be sure and pick up every single scrap of those nasty shingles! I'm sorry you're out of water. You can get a drink from my nasty garden hose and be sure you turn the faucet off tight. Blah, blah, blah."

We kids played up in the bed of his big roofing ruck and felt incredibly special indeed, way up there. When my middle brother got old enough, he sometimes joined Dad on the job, learning the trade for himself, helping lighten the work and sharing a sense of camaraderie.

The time came eventually when Dad told the boss, "No more high or steep roofs. I just can't handle them anymore." Then, it would be no more roofs at all, but rather inside carpentry work. And at last, a well-deserved retirement.

One of his arthritic knees would hardly bend anymore due to the years of his sitting with it tucked under him as he nailed shingles. His hips had suffered damage. And on the top of his hammer holding wrist, an unhealing sore developed. The malignant legacy of years in the sun, earning a living. The silent, deadly, gradual spread to nose, spine, and brain. The melanoma which, combined with age and tiredness, would take him from this world and home with the Lord and his beloved wife of many years.

My sister raised her head to look at us, as she clutched the folded American flag to her chest. "He's home now," she quietly said.

The funeral was ironically a happy one as we all sang, "When we all get to heaven, what a day of rejoicing that will be…" accompanied by family musicians on their various instruments. A daughter played piano, a son guitar. Another son sang tenor. I supplied the alto. My sister clung to the flag. The gathering was untraditional, but as unique as Dad was. If he could see us, I am sure he enjoyed it.

And stories, yes. The old army tales were retold over the funeral luncheon, which was comprised of his favorite foods, which family and friends had cooked and carried in. Memories shared amidst tears of love and loss. Loss of my father, and of the many loved ones others had known and treasured, now gone from us. Memories of beauty shared from lives well lived. Rest in peace, dear ones.

Beauty for Ashes

1. The ashes of death. The loss of our loved ones, and our missing them, lingers long. Take a moment to remember someone who illustrates the concept of "a life well lived." Why did you select that person? What do you remember most about them, and how did they impact your life?

2. Have you any special memories of God's comfort during times of great sorrow? How did he manifest His beauty and peace to you? Did he use other people to comfort you? Who? What did they do that touched your heart?

Scripture Reflection: "Precious in the sight of the Lord is the death of His saints" (Ps. 116:15).

God deeply understands the sorrow of death and loss. How might this verse illustrate his compassion toward us?

Prayer Thought: "Our Father, death and loss sear our hearts very deeply, and while we learn to cope, it seems the pain lingers for such a long time. Give us comfort and peace as we journey through life on this Earth. Amen."

Father and the Fiery Furnace

If we are thrown into the blazing furnace, the
God we serve is able to deliver us.

—Daniel 32:17

To my childish mind, it was the gateway to hell. My mental visualization when, in Sunday school, the place of punishment was mentioned. Besides being fiery, a living presence, it existed "down there," in the bowels of our home. In the gloomy dungeon known as the "furnace room." Next to it, restrained by a concrete block wall, crouched a jumble of black, dully glistening, lumpy coal. Waiting, just waiting. The fuel of hades.

I, as a youngster, would not enter the opening between the two block walls and into the room. No. No way. Occasionally, if I happened to be in the basement, I'd catch a glimpse of the glowing, flaming maw of the furnace if my father had the door open. It gave me nightmares. The furnace, the fiery furnace. The pulsing, consuming heart of our home. I hated it.

Back in the days of my childhood, most every house in town harbored a fiery furnace. Oh, a few more fortunate citizens boasted of a big heating oil tank on the property, complete with direct automatic feed into the furnace, making for less work and cleaner basements. Conversely, some of the less fortune households continuously struggled to build and maintain a wood pile, from which they endlessly split firewood to feed into glowing wood-burning stoves which radiated heat into the living quarters. For the most part, though, fiery furnaces were it.

Most every day, a big ole coal truck lumbered up a neighborhood street to make a delivery nearby. Coal chutes ran from truck to basement coal room windows, and grimy workers shoveled or otherwise transferred the load from truck to house. Usually, depending on the type of coal, a billow of gray black dust hung over the scene. More than once, a neighbor who had forgotten about the "coal truck coming" warning scurried frantically to get clean, drying laundry off the clothesline as the dusty fog spread through the area. High drama on a dull day!

As the empty truck drove off, the coal waited, hunkered down until the times of sacrifice. For the fiery furnace was, indeed, a place of sacrificial giving. My father was our primary acolyte. The guardian of the flame, which was to never go out. Throughout the day, as needed, my mother would descend the stairs into the basement and enter the fearful area. Gingerly, with a protective mitten on her hand, she would stand to one side and cautiously open the fearsome door. She would get a heap of coal on the coal shovel and push it carefully into the glowing depths of the fire. Once an adequate amount had been fed to the monster, she closed the door and with a sigh of relief, headed back upstairs.

At night, the fire would be unfed and allowed to burn low, as the family nestled under warm quilts, snug in their beds as the rooms slowly grew colder. Burn low did not, however, mean die out. A measured amount of coal would be added, then the day's ashes were raked over them and piled up, so the glowing embers could brood, wink, and hunker down all night. Waiting, just waiting.

Come early on often bitterly cold winter mornings, the true sacrifice began. The fiery furnace must be brought roaring into life before the children's feet hit frigid floors. Shivering, my father dressed in his flannel lined jeans, wool flannel shirt, wool socks, heavy work boots, and trudged down to the shrine room. When he opened the door, the orange-red banked ashes glowered at him, just waiting to roar into life. "Feed us," they demanded. "Feed us the life-sustaining coal."

Raking the ashes lightly, my father brought sparks to life as a small flare of flames blazed upward. Carefully he fed in new coal. Too much at once, and the feeble flames would be snuffed out. Licking eagerly at its breakfast, the fire strengthened and blazed anew. More coal! More heat!

Satisfied, my father securely fastened the door and placed the coal shovel where it would be handy for my mother to use later in the day when refueling was required. Dusting off his hands, he headed upstairs where warm air was rising into cold bedrooms. A hearty breakfast, hot coffee, and he would be off to work, knowing that out the ashes, warmth for his treasured family seeped into every corner of the house. The satisfaction beautifully blessed his mind.

Beauty for Ashes

1. My father sacrificed comfort every day by arising early and stoking the furnace. Have you experienced a similar incident of unsung faithfulness on the part of another? Ponder what they did and how it affected you. If possible, reach out to them and let them know what their efforts meant.

2. Often, seemingly fearful, painful, and trying events lead to positive results and blessings. If you have experienced such times, consider how they have ultimately benefited you and others.

Scripture Reflection: "If we are thrown into the blazing furnace, the God we serve is able to deliver us" (Dan. 32:17).

Has God delivered you from your fiery furnace—a seemingly impossible circumstance? How?

Prayer Thought: "Father, I truly hate pain and suffering. The dull aches of loss, loneliness, and hard times. Help me, Lord. Ease the sorrow and fill me with gratitude and trust that through such times, I grow in you. Amen."

Just Call Him Stew

He that hearkens unto counsel is wise.

—Proverbs 12:15

I had not been home to visit my family at the country home place for nigh onto a year and was, understandably, eager to see my parents, younger sister, and catch up on family news. It was after dark when I pulled into the driveway, but they had left the outdoor lights on for me. Happily, I walked up to the kitchen door and went in, pausing to breath in the familiar smells, sighing with joy.

"Hey, anybody home?" I called.

"She's here," said my younger sister, racing into the room to hug me. My mom followed, all smiles and hugs. Dad shook my hand and clapped a welcoming arm around my shoulders.

After the greetings, as I stowed my gear in my old bedroom, Dad popped his head in. "Did you have any problems getting from the car to the house?" he asked. Seemed like an odd question.

"Well, no. The sidewalk was well lighted. My drive went well, and I'm just so glad to be here."

"Good, and good to have you here. We missed you. If you get up and out early in the morning, there's a baseball bat leaning on the wall by the back door. Just carry that with you. So glad to have you here…" We went to join the others in the living room, deep in conversation.

Come morning, I, indeed, was up before anyone else, eager to stroll around the property in the early morning light, visit my favorite spot by the creek, and see both the familiar and the new. My, my, there was a baseball bat leaning on the wall by the back door! How strange. I saw absolutely no reason whatsoever to lug a ball bat around, so I just shrugged and walked out into the lovely summer morning.

Ah, it was so good to walk through the dew sprinkled yard as the dawn awakened. Birds flitted among the branches of the mulberry tree down by the hedge. The hedge itself, made up of wild rose bushes, smelled heavenly. The water in the creek splashed and gurgled over the rocks, and the vegetable plants in mom's garden showed robust growth. Beans, squash, and—YELP! OUCH! My leg had just been viciously and painfully stabbed. Then another mighty blow on my other leg. So much for wearing shorts. Ouch, the next blow really hurt! What in the world!?

My dad's voice rang out from the porch. "Run," he yelled. "Come on, just run. I'm coming to the rescue!"

One more vicious stab convinced to run now, question later. I ran toward the house. My dad, baseball bat in hand, ran toward me. "Keep going," he shouted, passing me by. Believe me I did, not looking back. I heard Dad shout a warning to whatever, I assume while waving the ball bat, and then my dad joined me on the porch.

"Come on, let's get your legs cleaned up and see if there's any real damage," he said, helping me into the house. I glanced back, looking for my attacker. There he stood, glaring at me. One really big, evil looking, angry White Leghorn rooster. A rooster! I did not know whether to laugh or cry.

"Dad, a chicken?"

"No, a rooster. Meanest son of a gun I've ever known, and I've known quite a few growing up on a farm. You should have carried the ball bat, you know," he chuckled.

"Yea, so it appears," I replied regretfully. My legs were red, and a bit wounded in spots, but nothing serious. "Could I ask, uh, why you keep that savage beast?"

"Well, he was supposed to be a hen like the other pullets we bought this spring. You know your mom likes her chickens. But then he grew up to be a rooster. Happens now and again. By then your sister and mom were kinda attached to him, and he is a handsome bird. Trouble is, the older he gets, the meaner he gets. Seriously, I think it's time for some chicken stew and dumplings around here. After this attack on you, I think they'll agree. Your sister just said the other day that her friends don't want to come over because they're scared of him."

When my mom and sister heard of my attack and saw my legs, the vote for chicken stew was four to zero. Now, just for the record, that rooster got the last laugh. The chicken stock was great, the veggies and dumplings quite edible, but nary a one of us actually ate any chicken. Chewing that tough bird was like chewing on rubber bands. Totally impossible. That was one tough rooster in every way.

Beauty for Ashes

1. Advice unheeded often has consequences. Recall and write of a time when you received good advice but ignored it. What was the advice? What were the consequences?

2. Sin can be a lot like that tough old rooster. So cute at the onset, beautiful as it grows, but ultimately turning into harmful ashes. Was there a "small" sin in your life that grew into something that just pecked at and wounded your soul? Explain what it was and how, eventually, it proved harmful. Have you been able to conquer it? How?

Scripture Reflections: "He that hearkens unto counsel is wise" (Prov. 12:15).

What is to be gained by listening to wise counsel?

Prayer thought: "Ah, Father, how often you warn us to be wise, to stay in your word, to trust in you but, thinking we know it all, your warnings are ignored. And then, the pecks and stabs of sin begin in our lives, and we must run to you yet again. Forgive us our foolishness, dear Lord, shelter us under your protective wings, and make something beautiful out of our lives. Amen."

The Great Kitten Giveaway

Surely you are one of them…then he began to call down
curses and swear to them, "I don't know the man."
—Matthew 26:73–74

I could just about literally see the smoke rising from my aunt's ears
and the daggers darting from her eyes. Fury, anger, disbelief oozed
from every pore, and she was rendered practically speechless. As in,
sputtering when she tried to talk. At her side, sobbing, clinging to
her hand, was a dear small child.

"But Uncle Mark said I could have a kitten! I want a kitty! I
want that kitty!" She pointed at a darling ball of orange fluff a few
feet away and started wailing anew. My aunt sputtered at a more
rapid rate, and finally managed to say "Here, you take her," to her
husband, place the child's hand in the hand of her dad, and stalk off
to the car. Door slam!

Whimpering, the little girl looked up expectantly at her father.
"Can I go get my kitty, Daddy?"

Sighing, knowing his wife might well throw him out of his
happy home, my uncle replied, "Yes, honey. Go get your kitty while I
see if your Uncle Mark has a box we can put her in to take her home."

Gleefully, the child scampered off and scooped up the orange
kitten. As it snuggled into the child's embrace, the little girl sighed
contentedly. "Oh, Daddy, I love her so much. Thank you, Uncle
Mark," she said as he brought a box over with a soft rag in it.

"Honey," her father instructed, "go take your kitty and get in
the car. Tell Mommy I said it's all right. I'm going to get some food
and litter for her, and then we'll go home."

My uncle waited until his daughter left and then turned around in anger. "Mark, I love you brother, but that was one thoughtless, cruel thing you did today. Telling all the little kids here at the family reunion they could take one of your kittens home, without checking with us parents first. What were you thinking? Not only my daughter, but look around at the other kids in tears as we're trying to load up and head home here. I know you thought you were being kind, making kids happy and finding homes for the kittens, but it wasn't kind. Crying kids. Distraught parents, some who may never speak to you again, for all I know. No, Mark. It was thoughtless and if you meant it to be funny, it isn't. We'll give the kitten a loving home, but still. Good night."

As families headed home, some with a new pet, others with sobbing kids, Mark's wife ran crying to the bedroom, overwhelmed with anger and humiliation. I observed from a distance on the porch, hurting for everyone involved. Mark stood dejected by the driveway, watching car taillights disappear into the night. Not the outcome he envisioned, I'm sure, and a sad ending to what had been, overall, a fun day.

Good intentions, all turned to bitter ashes at day's end and beyond. Several of the relatives did, indeed, decide to cut his family off for quite a while. Trust betrayed; relationships damaged. Yes, the intentions were good. And is not that often the case. We do not mean to hurt someone by our words or actions, but sometimes that is what we end up doing. Mouth in gear before the brain engages. That is we humans.

It reminds me of Simon Peter as Jesus was being arrested. "You are one of them!" the servant girl declares, pointing at Peter in the courtyard as Jesus was being taken away.

"No, I don't know him!" Peter avows with, finally, curses and oaths, driven possibly by a desire to do what seemed a good thing—to save himself from arrest. And Jesus looked at him as the rooster crowed, breaking Peter's heart.

God, in his grace, gave Peter beauty for ashes, forgiving him and eventually embracing him back into fellowship. God, in his grace, put forgiveness in the hearts of Mark's family members as eventually fellowship was restored. In fact, many of the various kittens grew into beloved family pets.

"Gotta tell ya, Mark," said my aunt who had been so furious that night. "Mad as I was the night of the reunion, I love that cat. She has been a dear companion to my daughter. I wouldn't talk to my husband for days, but now I can't imagine life without Ms. Ginger. Turned out to be a real blessing, you scoundrel you. Just don't you *ever* do anything like that again! Time for me to get going, but I wanted you to know it turned out okay." She gave Mark a hug, waved, got in her car, and drove away. Mark's expression at being forgiven, and even thanked, said it all.

Beauty for Ashes

1. Have you experienced the pain of good intentions gone awry, either as the giver or receiver of the action? What happened? Who got hurt and how?

2. Were things eventually set right? How did that come about? Did something good come out of the situation? Why or why not?

Scripture Reflection: "Surely you are one of them…then he began to call down curses and swear to them, 'I don't know the man'" (Matt. 26:73–74).

In your opinion, why did Peter deny Jesus as he did? Was he in any way justified? Might you have reacted the same way in a comparable situation? Have you, in fact, ever denied Jesus to save yourself from embarrassment or ridicule?

Prayer thought: "Dear Father, I am heartbroken at the too-frequent times my good intentions caused someone grief or sorrow. Forgive me when I am thoughtless, not thinking before I speak. Help me to be more sensitive to Spirit's guiding in all things. Amen."

Rabies or Babies?

I will entreat the Lord.

—Exodus 8:29

Here I sit atop a huge round bale of freshly cut hay in an Indiana hayfield, with a snarling, raging mama racoon down below, her little front paws braced against the hay. *Can raccoons climb?* I thought. Duh, I think they can. Don't they climb trees to get away from baying coon dogs and hunters? This is not looking good. Not at all. And don't they carry rabies? Yes, I believe they do. Yes, indeedy. On the bright side, I know, I think, her motive for rampaging after me across the field. I inadvertently startled her with her babies. Evidently, they were merely enjoying the sun, as was I, when I rounded a hay bale and…there they were.

I stopped in my tracks and looked at her. She stopped in her tracks and looked at me, looked back at her babies, looked at me more intently, and then took several steps in my direction. Quietly, I slowly took several steps backward. She took more steps toward me; I backed more steps away to indicate I was not interested in hurting her babies. Obviously, she did not believe me, not one second.

Did you know raccoons can make growling sounds? Trust me, they can. She did. Her speed picked up. Okay, I *know* you are not supposed to turn your back on a wild animal coming at you, but there goes that. I turned. I *ran* for all I was worth, wildly wondering where I could possibly go for safety in the treeless field. Round bale! That is all there was, baby!

Up I scrambled, digging hands and feet into the hay, and hoisting myself to the very top. Perched at least six feet off the ground, panting, I cautiously peered over the side, hoping to see nothing.

Uh-oh…she was definitely there, staring up at me, snarling. Maybe if I sat very, very still, she would go away. Wow, it seemed to work as after about seven hours (truly more like seven minutes) she snorted, dropped her front paws to the ground, turned around and headed back to her babies. I have never been so thankful for mother instinct!

Having decided to wait a good while before climbing down, in the hopes she and the kids would be truly gone from the field, I had time to quietly meditate. The blue cloudless sky above, a comfortable temperature, round bales stretching out into the distance, the scent of the newly mown hay. Hum. Interesting place to be. I can honestly say I had never, ever before, spent time atop a round bale.

God seemed remarkably close as I thanked Him for my deliverance from one of his creatures. Now that she was gone, I hoped, I could appreciate the fact that she was just protecting her little ones. How amazing are the animals on the Earth, in the seas, up in the air. The variety astounds. The more we study them, observe them, and respect them, the more in awe we are of their intelligence and interactions with their world.

Interacting with God's creatures brings us many lessons in life, many learning experiences. The more domestic animals share our lives, serve us, provide us with food, and ease our loneliness. Wild animals enthrall us, intrigue us, frighten us, and often baffle us. And the variety! What an amazing God who could come up with so many diverse types of life forms, all functioning in their own environments. If you ponder it, the realization comes that God made many of his creatures "just because," for his enjoyment. Until modern times, with our advanced methods of deep-sea exploration, thousands of "weird," beautiful, most unlikely creatures lived in the ocean depths where no human could see them. They were not evidently created for us but for God's enjoyment and purposes.

As I sat and meditated on God's creation, watching the birds (they kind of looked like vultures, actually, wheeling in circles above where I sat) the majesty of God as creator settled deep into my heart. The Bible says the day will come, in the new heaven and new Earth, when the lion will eat straw, lie down with the lamb, and there will be no fear, only peace. The enmity between creatures will be gone, over and done with. Perhaps we will even be able to freely communicate with one another, sharing love and joy. Something to think about and look forward to with hope. God surely loves his creatures, his creation.

Time had passed, the sun was sinking lower in the sky, and it was time to bravely climb down off the round bale and carefully head back to my parents' home, where I was visiting for a week. I stayed out in the open, careful not to suddenly "pop around" a bale, and I watched for any signs of raging raccoons. All was quiet. Possibly she and her brood were down at the stream, finding and opening mussels for their dinner. Arriving at the house, I opened the door to greet my mom and dad. "Hey, what's for dinner? Can I help?"

Beauty for Ashes

1. Often, it is when we are in a tight spot that our thoughts think to entreat the Lord through prayer. Describe a situation where you cried out for God's attention!

2. In the New Heaven and the New Earth, what do you envision things will be like?

Scripture Reflection: "I will entreat the Lord" (Exod. 8:29).
In what ways have you entreated the Lord lately? Have your prayers been answered yet?

Prayer Thought: "Father, here in this imperfect world, barriers hamper our understanding and communication between us and your magnificently created creatures. I praise you, Lord, that when you make all things new, these barriers will fall. Amen."

Broken

I sit here by the window,
and I look up to the sky.
I find myself asking, "Lord,
why the pain and sorrow?
The loneliness inside?"

I sit beside the window
as tears begin to roll.
They roll on down my cheeks;
I fear they will overflow.
My broken spirit can't mend.

Help me understand your ways,
and the meaning for the pain.
Let me understand, for I know
your love is real. I just don't understand—
How am I supposed to feel?

How do I accept what is
and what I may become?
Help me to remember
your love is with the one
whose heart aches.

And pains for my dear and loving son.
Lord, help us see your ways, Lord,
Lord, please continue to help.
Help me understand.
What does the future hold for us?

A life apart or close?
I listen and wait for your answer, Lord.
I listen and pray each day.
Lord, give me patience and a loving heart.
In Jesus's name, I pray.

Elizabeth M. Roberts

I'll Sort It Out

I shall go softly all my years.

—Isaiah 38:15

Piles of my parents' clothes surrounded me on the double bed, with more shirts, slacks, and dresses still on hangers in the closets. August morning sunlight diffused into the bedroom, promising a pleasant day. I had started this task of sorting through my deceased parents' garments the previous night by the dim light of a ceiling fixture, with darkness outside, and sorrowing darkness in my heart. A lifetime. These clothes chronicled a lifetime.

After parents die, someone needs to tackle the task of sorting clothing and prepping the house for what lies ahead. Since I was the out-of-town sibling staying at the family homestead during that funeral week, it seemed logical for me to sort the clothes, make decisions, box for charity, and throw away. Mom died in March; Dad passed in August. Within six months, both were at home with the Lord. I would not wish them back into their aged, worn-out bodies, but oh, how I missed them.

I lovingly held a simple yet elegant blue dress in my hands. Mom's "mother of the bride" and other special occasions go-to outfit. Weddings, anniversaries, special days at church warranted her donning this treasured garment. Lovingly, I folded it and laid it in the "to charity" box, blessed with memories of laughter, happy faces, and better times.

Soiled, stained T-shirts, both Mom's and Dad's, lay in a heap. Worn out by repeated wear and casual laundering at their nursing home facilities. Stains of soup splashed from spoons held by trembling fingers. Of catsup and mustard that oozed from the back of much enjoyed, if messy, hamburgers. And probably stained by tears shed when no one was around in the dark of night. All destined for the throw away box, along with memories of patiently hand-feeding Mom or Dad during visits. Tears. Lay the shirts in the box, along with tears.

Most of the blue jeans had holes in the knees, and they weren't artfully slashed in "designer jean holes," either. Dad's work jeans. Threadbare, worn and faded by the relentless hot sun shining on rooftops, where Dad labored to lay shingles in order to feed his family. Holes worn through knees scraping on singles as he, kneeling, worked his way from top ridge to gutters, pounding nails. Grit on the shingles; grit in his heart.

"These jeans should be enshrined," I thought. "But seriously, no. Like you, Dad, their lifetime is over, and they are just worn out." Into the throw away box they went.

Slowly, the sun shifted, and the room slipped into twilight as I steadily worked, having taken only a short break for lunch. I had taken my sandwich and chips to the backyard, where I sat overlooking the mowed green back acre and my parents' beloved vegetable garden area, sadly unplanted this year. My parents had seemed very close by, yet so far away. Then, back to work. As dusk fell, unutterable weariness set in. Pushing the remaining stacks aside, I arose, went to the kitchen for a bite of supper to eat, and then settled into Dad's chair in the silent living room. The walls seemed to close in; the loneliness threatened to overwhelm my soul. Here they sat, Dad in this chair reading his beloved western novels; Mom in her chair working on her current jigsaw puzzle.

Come bedtime, I ventured upstairs to "my" room, where its picture window allowed me to look out on the heavens while lying on the bed. I gazed at the brilliant moon and stars. Tears slipped down my face, and my heart ached. Alone, alone in the house. Memories of hustle, bustle when five children lived there. The gentle peace when it was just Mom and Dad, welcoming me on visits. And now…emptiness. Within days, dumpsters would arrive, and my siblings and I would begin clearing out and cleaning up. Throwing away a lifetime of that which was, is no more, and will never be again. The moon and stars shone brightly as I slipped into exhausted slumber.

Beauty for Ashes

1. What memories, if any, do you have of sorting through departed loved one's belongings, making decisions, and thinking of times past? Though difficult, how did that time of quiet reflection serve as a blessing? What conflicting emotions did you experience?

2. When memories come rushing in, good or bad, how do you react? How do you cope with what can be so difficult? Why did you select this coping method? If you still struggle mightily with overwhelming emotions, what might you do to help you deal with them?

Scripture Reflection: "I shall go softly all my years" (Isa. 38:15). What is this lovely scripture saying to you? What do you think it means?

Prayer Thought: "Great God, designer of the universe and of human emotions, be merciful to us in our times of sorrow. Wrap us with your great peace, and plant your hope in our hearts, lest we give up in despair. Thank you, Father. Amen."

Of Hummingbirds and Chemotherapy

The season of singing has come; the cooing of doves is heard.
—Song of Solomon 2:12

Deidre was alone. Not for one, two or three of her six chemotherapy appointments, but for all of them. Strictly speaking, there were people around her in the spacious chemotherapy room. Other patients. Medical personnel. Her designated nurse, who would administer the lifesaving drugs.

"Given we don't know how you will react, you must have someone drive you home after the first appointment. If all goes well, after that you can drive yourself," explained her oncologist during the pretreatment consultation.

Fearful and trembling, she explained the protocol to her husband over dinner. "Can you take me for the first one, stay with me, and bring me home?" she asked softly.

"What day?" he queried.

"My six treatments will be on Monday mornings at ten o'clock and will take about ninety minutes or so."

"Mondays? I'm sorry, but you know I must work, and Mondays there is always a backlog from the weekend. Tell you what. See if you can get one of your friends to take you, okay? Nice dinner," he said, rising from the table to go catch the evening news.

No reassuring hugs? No inquiries about the procedure? No asking about her feelings and fears? Head down, she stared at her dirty plate, where a tear plopped amidst the gravy. Who could she ask to take her and bring her home next week for the first appointment? He can't miss work, you know.

Fortunately, a friend happily agreed to take her, and thereafter Deidre drove herself without a problem. The cancer center offered supportive counseling, so she set up several sessions, hoping to assuage her fear and grief.

"Why," she sighed, "is my husband being so unsupportive? I've always been there for his various illnesses and surgeries, but now, in my greatest hour of need, he's 'got to work.' I don't understand this. Along with cancer, I'm trying to deal with anger, rejection, and bewilderment. What is going on? He simply won't discuss it with me."

"Keep in mind he's not my client," cautioned the counselor, "but I've been at this job for quite a while, and I've seen this more often than you would suspect. Going by my years of experience, I would venture that he is terribly frightened at the situation, at possibly losing you, at the disruption in his life's routine."

"Frightened? *He's* frightened? Like I'm not? He's frightened, so he abandons me?"

"I could be wrong, mind you. But as I said, I've seen this reaction more times from spouses than you'd imagine. He may feel helpless in the face of your suffering and possibly dying. He's used to you caring for him, rather than he caring for you when it comes to everyday chores and household routine. Frankly, he doesn't want that familiar routine changing and of course, that major question of how this will impact your lives in the future if things don't go well remains. I suspect it's all too much for him to face, so his go-to response is deny and ignore. What do you think?"

Deidre sighed heavily. "I don't know, and frankly, even if that is the cause of his behavior, it still hurts me, and it still boils down to the fact it's all about him. I may understand better, but I'm still hurt beyond belief."

"Understandable. I'm a Christian man with strong faith in God, and if you're comfortable with it, I'd like to pray with you as we end our session," he quietly offered.

"Yes," Deidre replied. "I'd like that." God's peace and grace filled her heart as the prayer was offered, and then she quietly gathered her belongings and left.

Once the strangeness and fears of the first chemotherapy treatment gave way to a more comfortable familiarity, Deidre immersed herself in the compassion of the staff and nurses. At each session, after selecting her complimentary beverage and snack, she settled into a recliner chair near the picture window, where outside myriad birds flitted to and from the feeders. Once the ordeal of "finding a usable vein for the intravenous needle" was over, she would settle back for a time of prayer and reflection.

"Father, thank you for the shapes and colors of your birds. They bring me such peace and joy. I love the little round gold finches at the sunflower feeder. They are precious. And the cheerful scarlet cardinals, the bossy blue jays. But, Father, my favorites are the hummingbirds sipping nectar. Such tiny mites, easy to overlook as they zoom by. One of the "least of these" among the bird world. Just what I feel like, sitting here as powerful medicine drips into my veins. A true "least of these" in the realm of humanity.

"How persistently the hummers hover at the feeder, enjoying the life-sustaining nectar, their wings beating so fast I can hardly see them. They give me courage, Lord. Truly they do. Just as I patiently sit here, soaking up medicine which will, hopefully, sustain my life, the tiny hummingbirds flit, flitter, and take in life-giving fluid. Hope, Father. Your kaleidoscope of birds gives me hope. Your eye is on the sparrow, so I know you are watching over me."

Treatment done, Deidre slowly walked over to the lounge area for a coffee and another snack. The importance of hydration and lots of calories was continually reinforced by the treatment team. "Relax and be sure all is well before driving home," they routinely admonished.

Hummingbirds. To this day, Deidre vividly recalls the peace of the tiny birds. In place of a supportive husband, the Lord sent His jeweled gift of colorful birds to strengthen her faith. The ashes of disillusionment replaced with the beauty of His feathered hope.

Beauty for Ashes

1. God sends us His messages of hope and encouragement in various ways. Recall an incident where, in times of trials and stress, something seemingly insignificant lessened your fear and restored your courage.

2. People can, indeed, let us down in many (often unexpected) ways. Give it some thought. What might motivate you, or someone else, to "not be there" for another person in need? How can we be aware of and work through such times?

Scripture Reflection: "The season of singing has come; the cooing of doves is heard" (Song 2:12).

Do you enjoy singing to the Lord? What are some of your favorite songs? If appropriate, burst out in song right now, raising your voice to God.

Prayer Thought: "Father, creator of all things great and small, forgive us when we deliberately or unknowingly fail those depending on us. You know we are but dust, but you, Father, can bring beauty from the ashes of our failings. Please be ever merciful toward us. Amen."

I Feel Your Presence

Open up my heart and mind
so I can feel you all around.
I am feeling oh so lonely
as I kneel upon the ground.

I feel so dark and empty
as your love for me abounds.
Lord, open up my heart and mind,
let my ears hear heavenly sounds.

I feel your gentle spirit.
I feel your sweet breath.
I hear your heavenly voice
as it takes away my stress.

I feel your arms around me.
I know my heart will see
your loving spirits as
you hold and comfort me.

My dear sweet Jesus,
my love I give to you.
My life I lift up to you,
for I have work to do.

Lead on, oh, Lord, and guide me
through each and every day.
That I may do your will, Lord,
with your help along the way.

Elizabeth M. Roberts

Behind Cell Bars

Continue to remember those in prison as if you
were together with them in prison.

—Hebrews 13:3

"Pray for me, please," the prisoner wrote on his Bible study answer sheet. "I am weary. I feel unbearably sad and discouraged. Yes, God has found me in this place, and I rejoice. I study his word and trust in him. How many prayers I've fervently prayed, that he would take me home to him. That I would go to sleep and not awake to another day in this cell. My poor choices put me here, and I thank God it did because I learned about the Lord here and became his child. If I were still on the outside, I'd probably be dead without Christ in my life. But I'm weary of it all. The ceaseless cursing and cussing. The mocking of my God and my faith by cellmates. Of being endlessly confined, especially with all the COVID 19 restrictions, and facing many more bleak years before me. I've tried to kill myself twice in the past; I believe I'll try again soon unless God takes me home. Lord, I believe. Help my unbelief. Pray for me. Thank you."

And so, I do. I pray for him. Oh, how I've prayed since I graded his lesson and dropped it in the mail to be returned to him. There is nothing else I can do. His mail is opened at the prison before he gets it, so hopefully someone will read what he wrote and get him help for his depression.

"Lord, wrap him and so many others of your imprisoned children in your peace and love. Hope, Father. Give them hope day by day. Give this specific person a reason to embrace life and serve you. Amen."

Until I began volunteering with a prison ministry that coordinates and facilitates Bible studies in prisons nationwide, I had absolutely no idea that prisons are such a flourishing, growing mission field for the Lord. Week after week, six or so lessons completed by inmates cross my desk for grading and comments. To say the least, it has been an eye-opener. The absolute number one comment written by the students is "Thank God I was sent to prison, or I would be without God in my life, and most likely dead."

Thank God for prison? Beauty for ashes. Out of bad, the Lord brings good for those who seek him. On the outside, many of these people were hopelessly mired in drug or other addictions. They were lost in a seemingly unbreakable bondage, where no amount of pleading or threats by loved ones, or painful results from their behavior, reached them.

"I've raped someone. I've murdered someone. I've stolen, broken into houses. I've peddled dangerous drugs, addicting even children." On and on, the litany of woe. And of course, there are those who avow they did nothing, but were wrongly convicted. Only God knows the truth of it. I certainly don't. But the point is, many have come to know the Lord, and that makes all the difference.

God uses them mightily on a mission field the non-incarcerated cannot enter, nor truly understand. Prisoners can often reach out to fellow prisoners, sharing the gospel and partnering in prayer. "I'm in for life," the Bible course student shared, "but my goal is to complete my theology degree and dedicate the rest of my life to serving the Lord. I want to minister to those who come through these gates, and I'm well on my way to achieving my goal."

As Paul was an apostle in chains, preaching the Good News, so are many of the incarcerated. Those of us who have a loved one in prison know the grief and sorrow incarceration causes. Grief and sorrow over the bad decisions made. Grief and sorrow at limited visitation and contacts. Grief and sorrow at seeing the loved one's children being reared by a now single parent or a stepparent. Did God want our loved ones sent to prison? Absolutely not, never. But it was allowed to happen. And in that place, for many, God's Spirit reached out to dear loved ones and drew them close to God's great love and grace. Further, many Christ followers behind bars are doing what they can to draw others to the joy found in Jesus and the promise of eternal life. God's people, rising up from evil, patiently attempting to lead others home to God's goodness. Pray, oh pray, for the prisoners.

Beauty for Ashes

1. Do you have someone in prison, or do you know of someone behind bars? Are they experiencing God's love and grace, or are they growing bitter and hardened? What might you do in either situation, as far as reaching out to them?

2. If the Lord so leads, consider researching the various prison ministries in existence, find out what they do / require, and perhaps consider volunteering. God will bless your efforts.

Scripture Reflection: "Continue to remember those in prison as if you were together with them in prison" (Heb. 13:3).

While you and I may not be physically in an actual prison, in what other ways do we or have we experienced bondage? Where should we go for comfort and freedom? How?

Prayer Thought: "Father, thank you for drawing so many who are 'in bondage' both literally and spiritually to you. Be with your precious children who labor for you within our prisons, often in the face of ridicule and possible danger. Amen."

Through the Woods

Across the wooden foot bridge. Through the woods, across the soccer field, past the park's playground to my car. Get in. Drive to work.

After work, park car in park's public lot. Get out and lock car. Walk past the playground, across the soccer field, through the woods. Across the wooden foot bridge. Arrive home. Next morning, repeat the quarter mile journey in reverse. For the next foreseeable mornings, in fact.

And so it went during that particularly difficult time in my life. Either do the routine, or awaken some morning to find my car gone, snatched by the repossession company. Daily, I hoped they would not see the car parked across the way, on the other side of the park. I always backed into the parking space, so the license plate was less visible. Life can, indeed, get interesting.

And no, I was not a dead-beat person trying to avoid making my car payments, regardless of what the nasty collection agents sneered on the phone. Frankly, it was either late car payments or late mortgage payments, and the mortgage payments would have been a lot harder to catch up on when things finally turned around. Some of you have been where I was, for sure. Some of you may be there now. You know what I am saying. You also know the pain, the shame, and the stress of a life that seems to have gone down in flames and turned into ashes.

The fact was, I had to hold onto the car to get to work, to get paychecks essential to meeting my bills. Hence, park across the park, walk home in the dark. Well, okay, I had a flashlight. But still.

It all started with an excellent job offer from a school district in another state. Nice school, interesting area to move to, and the grade levels I most enjoyed teaching. After considerable discussion, my husband and I put our property up for sale in preparation for relocating. Did I mention we would be leaving the often-miserable winter climes in western Pennsylvania for the relatively balmy environs of eastern North Carolina? Ah, an added incentive for sure.

Packed, details arranged, move date set, affordable house lined up in our new city for when we arrived—we were good to go. And then the phone call came. The devastating, unbelievable phone call. "We are so sorry, and we regret to inform you that the special funding we counted on for several of our upcoming classroom hires has been unexpectedly withdrawn. Needless to say, making this call to you and the others on such short notice before the beginning of the fall term distresses us greatly. I am so, so sorry, but you no longer have a position."

It stresses *him* greatly? I am the one all packed up, locked and loaded for relocation to another state quite a distance away. After many tears and considerable discussion, we decided to make the move anyway. My husband had a job lined up down there, though at a modest wage, and hopefully I would find a teaching position in the remaining weeks before the new term started. So we did. We made the move.

And I did not find a teaching position on such short notice. As the realization and reality sank in, I bit the bullet, acknowledged I would need to seek non-teaching employment for this semester, and possibly this school year, and accepted I would not be using that hard won teaching degree in the foreseeable future. Are we down hearted? Yes, yes, yes.

After persistent job searching for any work remotely related to my English major degree, the most welcome telephone call came. "We would like to offer you the position of full-time proofreader at our law firm. Your English skills are excellent, and your references gave you good reports. If you want the job, it's yours. Welcome aboard."

If I want the job! An interesting office environment, using the skills I was taught? Yes, just yes! It was such an appreciated blessing, and I was gratified beyond words. However, the salary was modest compared to what I had planned on when we moved, so penny pinching would be required. The move had been expensive, the interval of my unemployment lengthy, and trying to catch up loomed ahead. No matter. I was extremely grateful, as was my husband. Let the penny-pinching begin! And that included parking across the way in the park, walking past the playground, across the soccer field, through the woods. Across the wooden foot bridge. Arrive home. Reverse in the morning. For as long as it would take.

Fortunately, it did not take all that long, once I got established in my new position, and we found a local charity food pantry to help us save on groceries. Paychecks began to come in. Slowly but steadily, things improved. When the evening came that I finally was able to park my car in our driveway, I was beyond happy. Be gone, quarter mile walks twice a day!

From the seeming ashes of that often heart-rendering experience came much beauty, truth be told. While I clearly remember the great pain from back then, that life event developed my capacity for compassion tremendously. How easy it is to be smug in one's cozy, safe, middle-class world, until it all unexpectedly falls apart. Jesus had such compassion for those experiencing life's difficulties, something the more fortunate can tend to lack at times. Those of us who have "been there, done that" hopefully develop the valuable beauty of understanding and caring about people trying to arise from the ashes life dumps on them. There, but for the grace of God, go we.

Beauty for Ashes

1. Reflect, possibly share, a grim time you endured in life's journey, whether in the past or now. What events led to the situation? How did you/are you coping with it? Did someone special help you?

2. Has there been an opportunity for you to work with, encourage, or otherwise assist someone experiencing financial, medical, or other life challenges? What did you do? What blessings and benefits have both you and the folks you helped/help gained?

Scripture Reflection: "Anxiety weighs down the heart, but a kind word cheers it up" (Prov. 12:25).

When you read this verse, what comes to your mind? An anxiety with which you struggle? Kindness you give or get? Pause to reflect and respond to these wise words.

Prayer Thought: "Lord, it is easy for us to pridefully think 'see what I've done, notice how great I am,' as we look down on those who 'could do better if they would just try.' Father, let us remember always that *you* give us every blessing, talent, opportunity, and ability we have, and that it can all disappear in a heartbeat. Teach us compassion and trust, as we walk our life's journey. Amen."

Bridging the Gap

Ask now the beasts, and they shall teach thee.

—Job 12:7

Halfway up the open, winding stairs leading to the fire tower "away up there," I froze. As in, "hand locked onto the stair railing, feet not able to move, eyes glazing over" froze. My so-called friends below me sniped, "Uh, could you get moving up there? You're holding up the line."

Hyperventilating, I whispered to my husband, "I've gotta get down. Can't move. Help me get down." Sighing, he peeled my fingers from the railing.

"It's really not that high, you know," he assured. Maybe not, but the problem wasn't entirely the up; it was the down. I could see all the way down through the steel grate stairs and unfortunately, I had looked down.

Once he got my fingers lose, my spouse put a hand on each shoulder and slowly turned me around and then put my hand on the railing. "I'll walk in front of you," he assured. "You won't fall."

Slowly, I baby stepped to the stair edge and started down. One step, two steps, three steps. Down, down, done. Well, I had tried to make it up. Fear of heights has long been a companion of mine, and it's quirky. Give me solid stairs and a sturdy guard rail, and I'm fine up on a roof, gazing over the city. Flying? No big deal as long as I'm seated over the wing or in the aisle seat, where I can't look straight down. Folks say, "Mind over matter," but the panic and muscle immobility that can strike when I do become frightened isn't easily overcome.

Still, hope springs eternal or, more precisely, ignorance is bliss. "I'm going to the Virginia mountains for a trail riding and camping weekend," the owner of the farm where I boarded my horse said. "It's an annual event at a beautiful location, and the main trail is really nice. It's an old railroad bed, where the railroad company pulled up the tracks and ties, smoothed it out, and then donated a section of the property to the state park it ran through. Now, the old railbed can be used for hiking, biking, and horseback riding. I've room to take several of you and your horses if anyone would like to go."

Sign me up! Sounds marvelous. Wide, smooth, designated trails. The kind of trails where I could let my Tennessee Walking Horse just open up and glide along at top speed. Ah, a perfect, relaxing weekend, for sure.

The group was loaded up early come Saturday morning, and we headed up the road to Virginia from North Carolina. Halfway to our destination, we and others heading to the same campground pulled into a restaurant for breakfast. After checking on the horses, we took time to talk with parents and kids who came over to the trailers, answering their questions and letting them pat inquisitive horse noses. That many horses always drew a crowd!

Fortified with breakfast, we hit the road again. Leaving the main highway, the big pickups wound their way higher and higher through the cool, shadowy forests until we reached the spacious campground. Quickly and efficiently, everyone parked trailers, unloaded horses, and saddled up, ready to head out on the trail.

"Mount up!" commanded the trail boss. We were off. It was a cool, gorgeous morning, the horses were full of energy, and what with the wide, smooth trail, everyone was able to relax, chat, and enjoy the views.

"Ah, life is good," I thought in a contented state of innocent bliss.

Do you know that in the mountains, trains must get from mountainside to mountainside by crossing over valleys? Yes, indeedy. And do you know how they cross over those valleys? Yes, indeedy. *They go over railroad trestles.* Long, long trestles, with only guard rails on the sides. Look over, and you can see all the way down to the valley below. Okay, now, yes. When they took out the tracks, they affixed wide, sturdy planking on the trestle itself, so you couldn't look directly down, but rest assured. Even from the center of the former track bed, you had no choice but to see the expanse of space on either side.

And just how were we riders to cross from this mountainside to the other mountainside on this trail ride? Of course. We were to ride our horses across the trestle, clip clopping over the wooden planking. Way up there in the air. I am going to die.

There were horses and riders both in front of me and behind me on the trail as we approached the trestle, and given the herd nature of horses, pulling my mount out of line, and going back to the campground would surely cause a disruption. Not to mention, I had no idea of the route back to camp.

"Breathe," I told myself. "Just breathe. Relax your fingers on the reins. Relax your body." Tears of fear streaked down my face. There was no recourse; I had to ride across the trestle. As I prayed, a still, quiet voice of instruction soothed my mind.

"Put the reins down on Pixiejoy's neck. Let go of the reins and rest your hands on the saddle horn. Set balanced in your saddle. Now—close your eyes."

Close my eyes!? Well, okay. I let go of the reins, laid them on her neck, balanced in the saddle, closed my eyes, and trusted my mount would patiently follow the horses in front of her and take care of me. Breathe in, breathe out.

Pixiejoy crossed the bridge quietly, each step making a hollow sound on the wood. Clip, clop. Clip, clop. Then, a step and only silence of hoof on loamy Earth. We were across. Breathing a prayer of thanksgiving, I picked up my reins and rejoined the land of the living. I crossed that long expanse with my eyes closed tight, blindly trusting that horse and the Lord. Thank you, Father!

Oh, and an even greater thanksgiving was mine when we took a different route back to camp—on totally solid ground. Yep, life was good.

Beauty for Ashes

1. Fear is real. Fear is powerful. If you can, close your eyes and revisit/visualize a time when you experienced great fear. What was it?

2. Have you since dealt successfully with that fear? If so, what helped you get through and overcome it? If not, what steps might you take to lessen or alleviate your distress?

Scripture Reflection: "Ask now the beasts, and they shall teach thee" (Job 12:7).

What life lessons has God taught you through interaction with His creatures, the animals?

Prayer thought: "Lord, Father and Protector, you totally understand our greatest fears, where they come from, and why they distress us so. Bless us with your presence, and guard us as we seek understanding and healing. Help us to totally trust in you. Amen."

Lay Her Down

For he guards the course of the just and
protects the way of his faithful ones.

—Proverbs 2:8

She was extraordinary in all the ways that mattered. Beautiful, patient, kind to the very core of her being. Very humble, with a knack for knowing what needed to be done, and then just quietly doing it. Not flashy, not a "showboat." Easily overlooked amidst those with more flash and dash. But faithful. Oh my. Absolutely faithful and trustworthy. You could depend on her for your life, and she wouldn't let you down.

She knew her job and when called upon, did it. She loved children, even when they got a bit too loud, rough, or rowdy. In fact, the day before she died, she was on the job working at the barn's annual summer horse camp. Going out on the trail in the woods, genuinely enjoying making the children happy. Oh, she was getting on in years, and she had to stop to rest and catch her breath a bit more often than usual, but given the camp leader, staff, and young attendees were not in any hurry, that was not a problem.

Her name was Leather, with lovely chestnut hair and soulful eyes filled with love. She was a good horse.

In all my thirty-plus years of teaching, I could count on one hand the times I woke up ill in the morning, necessitating calling off work and requesting a substitute. That memorable day was one of those rare occasions. I felt absolutely terrible, with a queasy stomach and overall fatigue. It pained me to dial the automated substitute system number, put in a request, and give directions as to where the emergency plans for the day were located. Ohhhhhhh. I just wanted to go back to bed.

I had just settled back in among my pillows when the telephone rang. Groggily, I sat up and answered the call.

"Sandra?"

"Yes?" It was the owner/manager of my horse's boarding stable.

"I'm glad I caught you before you left for work. I hate to say it, but Leather could barely walk up from the pasture this morning. I had to coax her, wait for her to stop and catch her breath, and then take a few more steps. I finally got her into the box stall, and I called her vet. Listen. Dr. Tom was out this way, so he came on over and examined her. He just left but said to try to reach you. Leather is in extreme heart failure, but she's comfortable. He knows how much you love that horse, so he wanted me to try to catch you and tell you if you can come to the barn in an hour or so, he'll meet you here. He's got a farm call down the road, and then he'll come back. He thought you might want to be here when he puts her down. I'm so sorry." Janet was softly crying; she loved Leather also.

"Heart failure! Put her down! Oh, Janet…I can't bear it, but it explains her lack of energy and heavy breathing at times lately. I'll be right over, soon as I get dressed."

As I prepared to head to the barn, it struck me that I didn't feel ill at all. No upset tummy or dizziness. It further struck me that if I'd gone into work, Janet would not have been able to reach me, nor would I have been able to leave work and get to the barn in time.

"Lord, I see Your hand in this! You brought this wonderful animal into my life years ago, when I wasn't even looking to own a horse. You let her sustain and comfort me through many unhappy situations, and you used her to bless the kids here each summer during horse camp. You, Father, know how much I love her, and how much she loves me. Lord, truly, I see your hand in this, that we can take this final journey together. Amen."

With a heavy heart, I pulled into the driveway and went to Leather's stall. Putting her halter on, I slowly led her out to the spacious yard under the pear tree, where a carpet of ground cover wildflowers was blooming. Not uncomfortable at all, she quietly munched on the sweet grass as I stroked her chestnut neck and gave her hugs. All too soon, the veterinarian's truck pulled in. Dr. Tom got out, carrying his medical bad, and came over to give me a hug. "I'm so sorry. We both love this mare more than we can say. She's been a one in a million special horse, and I mean that. It's a blessing that the heart failure is causing her no suffering or pain as long as she's quiet and doesn't exert herself. Before we begin, let me explain what will happen. We can do everything right here, amidst the wildflowers. What could be more perfect? I'll be giving her a first shot, and within seconds, she'll want to lie down. Just let her. When you're ready emotionally, let me know, and I'll give the fatal shot. I want you to know she might thrash about, not in pain but because of muscle reactions, so stay alert. Are you ready?"

Ready? How does one get ready for losing one of life's most wonderful, faithful friends? "Yes," I said. A gentle spring breeze caressed us and the flowers. Dr. Tom proceeded, and my girl slowly and gently laid down. I sat on the grass amidst the flowers with Leather's beautiful head cradled in my lap. Her eyes slowly closed, and she nickered at me in peace as I stroked her nose.

"I'm ready," I told Dr. Tom. He gave her the final shot. There was no thrashing about of any kind, only deep peace as her breathing became slower and slower until it stopped. She was gone. I sat there for several minutes, just stroking her neck. Then, arising, I paid and thanked Dr. Tom and with one backward, longing goodbye, got in my car and left. The farm owner later on would dig a grave with the backhoe, and gently lay her body in it. Later that spring, I planted a lovely red rose bush over her grave, in memory.

The ashes of a great love gone, though the memories remain. Times of joy, both for myself and others who loved and rode that marvelous horse. "Oh, Father, how I will miss her!" my heart cried out.

"Yes," whispered the gentle voice of Spirit, "and how very blessed you were to know and love her. She was my gift to you, the horse you always wanted from the time you were a little girl. The horse you thought you would never, ever have in your lifetime. A beautiful horse, with a giving, beautiful spirit. Because I love you, my child. I blessed you with a great desire of your heart. Her death leaves your heart in ashes right now, but the beauty of her life will always remain in the minds and hearts of so many. Peace. My peace I give to you."

Beauty for Ashes

1. God knows the deaths of beloved animals and people hurts us so, but he allows it anyway. What are your thoughts on this? What helps deal with the pain?

2. It is said that the depth of our grief reflects the depth of our love. Do you agree or not? Why or why not?

Scripture Reflection: "For he guards the course of the just and protects the way of his faithful ones" (Prov. 2:8).
Do you find this to be true in your life? If so, in what ways.

Prayer Thought: "Our Father, you give us so many blessings in life, including the ability to love. And yet, Father, loving greatly causes so much pain throughout our lives. However, Father, we know your love is perfect and limitless, and that you will take away all pain and sorrow when we go to live with you. Thank you, Lord, for your great love. Amen."

Crushin' It

I will put enmity between you and the woman and between your offspring and hers. He will crush your head; you will strike his heel.

—Genesis 3:15

"The best way to grow is to get out of your comfort zone," *they* say. Well, self, get ready for a growth spurt because discomfort lies ahead. This somewhat sheltered lady "of a certain age" is taking her first solo soiree to the junk yard.

No, wait. Off to a bad start already. *Not* junk yard. The ecologically aware, environmentally sound recycling center. There. Got it. So okay, adventure lies ahead. Let me exhibit nerves of steel, a backbone of iron, with copper-clad courage. I'm gonna be crushin' it!

It all began with the necessity of downsizing from a two-story house with finished basement to a twelve thousand something square foot ranch house. Unfortunately, the most logical project to tackle first was clearing out said basement of accumulated cast-off electronics, old broken tools, reems of unused wire, various cans with enough screws and nails to build several house, and similar valuable—*ahem*—items.

A tentative phone call to the recycler's elicited instructions to "Just load your cast offs in boxes and bring them over. We'll show you what to do." Not having a pickup truck, I loaded my car trunk and back seat as tightly as possible. It became apparent this project would require several trips. No matter. A long journey begins with the first small steps, so into the trunk went obsolete VCR machines, moldy stereo speakers, receivers from the "good old days," nonworking television sets (and we're not talking flat screens here.) Boxes of copper cored wires went in. "We'll pay more if you strip the wires before bringing them," the recyclers said. Like I wanted to spend hours stripping rubber casings off the copper!

An attempt to close the trunk led to more re-arranging. Try, try again. Finally, off I went, with a good deal of apprehension. I had a distinct gut feeling I was about to enter an alien world; I was right. Pulling into the recycler's spacious driveway, I positioned my small passenger car into a line going who knew where. It was obviously the thing to do. Pickup truck, appliance store truck loaded with beat-up stoves and washing machines, pickup truck, big old flatbed truck hauling various car engines, older lady in passenger car (me!), behemoth dump truck. You get the picture. All accompanied by the noise of diesel engines and crushing machines clanging away.

Furthermore, it was just me and the guys. As in men. Stop. Go. Stop. Go. At last, I rounded the corner and, at the urging of the man waving me on, drove onto the scales and got my official ticket to hold onto and eventually carry into the cashier's office to collect whatever my treasures were deemed worth. That was not too difficult!

Around the next corner, I realized it was time to back my car into one of the many narrow unloading bays. Backing was not my strong suit, even when unstressed. All around me, piles of crushed metal rose into the sky. Cranes steadily picked up wrecked cars and swung them into position for the giant crushers to take them from three dimensional to two dimensional. Flat as pancakes.

Semitrucks backed up, filling the air with screeching beeps and shrieks. Occasionally, a load broke loose from a crane and came crashing down, shaking the Earth. And the two guys waving at me in my rearview mirror wanted me to back into the unloading shed. Honestly, I tried. Frantic waving in my mirror and shouts of "No, no. Otra vez!" did not help. I knew enough Spanish to try, try again. Finally, probably in self-defense, one of the workers came to the driver's door and gestured for me to get out. Deftly, he eased the car into perfect position, popped the trunk, indicated where I was to wait, and they began to sort through my offerings.

Frankly relieved, I stood and waited while he and a partner categorized and weighed the various metals, wires, and electronics. Once finished, they indicated I was to get in, drive through the next gate, and wait at the cashier's office. They would compute my ticket and hand it to the cashier. That, I could manage.

As I awaited my turn at the window, I pondered the experience. Seemingly endless stacks of metal being crushed, smashed, changed in form. Once new, useful vehicles, appliances and assorted other items which had reached the end of their lives. It was time for them to be crushed and transformed into metal sheets that could then be resurrected to create new, recognizable objects. Someone, some-where, would take all this rusty, ruined, useless "junk" and turn it into things of worth and beauty.

"How like us," I pondered. God, through Jesus, takes our worn, filthy, rusted, selves made useless by sin, and He crushes us. That can be messy, noisy, painful, and confusing. He tells us to let go, deny ourselves, and trust him as he takes us through our recycling. Our spirits will rise anew as God's children, never again to be sep-arated from Him. And some day, even our worn-out bodies will be "recycled" into splendid, eternal spiritual bodies. He will, and does, promise to give us beauty for ashes. Always.

Beauty for Ashes

1. Recall, and hopefully laugh, at a time or situation where you obviously did not blend in. What was it? How did you feel? What did you learn from it?

2. Just for the joy of it, as we cannot currently know for sure, speculate what you think our someday spiritual bodies will be like. What age will we eternally be? Appearance? Will they be something totally different from what we are now? What biblical "clues" can you think of.

Scripture Reflection: "I will put enmity between you and the woman, and between your offspring and hers. He will crush your head; you will crush his heel" (Gen. 3:15).

God from the beginning had a plan to crush Satan and his evilness by sending Jesus for our redemption. In what way has Satan struck Jesus's heel? How did Jesus crush Satan?

Prayer thought: "Lord, you continually grow us by putting us in challenging, unfamiliar places and situations. Be with us, Father, for it is hard for us humans to be uncomfortable and feel alien. Give us the strength to learn and experience all you desire for us as we journey home to you, and continually remind us that Satan has, indeed, been crushed. Amen."

Pieces

I am broken.
I see the pieces of who I am lying all around me.
Where do I begin to find them,
to start putting them back together?

What if a few pieces are lost?
What if a piece or two are gone—
can I still fit back together?

Lord, you are the center piece,
and the border
holding me all together.

Without you, God, I will
continue to be in pieces.
God, you are the master builder.

You are the creator; you put me all together.
You knew me before I was
in my mother's womb.

You have woven every intricate detail
of my being. And only you
can help put me back together.

Piece by piece.
You will twist and turn each one to fit.
Putting me back to how you want me to be.

ASHES IN THE CLOSET

You know who I am.
You know who you want me to be.
I am yours, God.

Build me. Piece me together
to be just who you want me to be.
Master Puzzle Maker.

You know how to put me together,
to make a beautiful picture—
of *me*!

Elizabeth M. Roberts

I'm Puzzled

It is the glory of God to conceal a matter.
—Proverbs 25:2

Thank you, new neighbor Pamela who absolutely adores jigsaw puzzles and gave me some which I took out of politeness and a desire to have something in common with her and I knew good and well my brain does not do puzzles. But after taking the puzzle, all three hundred puzzling pieces, I was stuck. After all, I had intimated that I enjoyed puzzles when talking to her. Upon which she said, "Wonderful. I have a whole stack of great puzzles. When you get this one together, take a photo of it on your phone and text it to me! I'll be so proud of you. Then you can bring it back and pick out another one."

Yikes. *Now* what do I do? This could go on for years! Talk about walking the walk, not just talking the talk. And thus, my newfound hobby of putting puzzles together began. Actually, I had dabbled in puzzles years ago when my mom was still living. She loved them, and in order to keep her company, I would sit with her in the living room, work on her current puzzle, and visit. In truth, she worked, and I put in a piece now and again if, by some lucky chance, I found one that fit somewhere. In my current situation, it was impossible to camouflage my lack of effort. There was no one but me, for the most part, putting it together.

Pam gave me some expert pointers. Lay out all the pieces, if possible, and arrange them by color. Pick out all the border pieces (they have at least one flat side) and then put the border together. Whew. Once I got that done, I felt positively inspired! Onward and upward. This isn't too bad; I can manage it.

Pick out one section to focus on, she suggested, rather than randomly jumping from area to area. If there was a defined object in the picture, like an animal or person, it could be helpful to start there. "Well," I'm thinking, "makes sense to me to work from the top down. That way, I can sort of lay some pieces in the center of the frame, giving me more room. This puzzle, my very first one, has a lovely blue sky with floating clouds in it. Looks nice. Let's do it."

Now I know all you experienced puzzle experts out there are shouting, "No, no, no. Don't do it!" But hey, what did I know. And that's where we almost—almost—got to literal ashes with my puzzle experience. I sat there. Light bulb burning away, clock ticking, time passing. And I looked at blue pieces that were all, well, various shades of blue. Or white pieces that were distressingly all—white.

When I lamented to Pam, she chuckled and said, "Okay, if you are determined to work from the top border down, you'll probably have to focus on shapes, not color."

That's when my lack of spatial detection skills became sharply evident. Honestly, I would look for the piece with two regular tabs and a spade-looking tab and not find it. Try the pieces by picking them up and attempting to put them in what little puzzle I'd completed. *None* of them seemed to fit. Now how could that be? And so it went, to the point where incineration seemed like the only solution.

What really was maddening, and I'm sure psychologists and such people have this all figured out, is I'd be about crying in frustration, turn out the light, leave the room, and forget about the wretched thing. Come the next morning I'd walk in the room, glance down, and *boom, boom, boom*, I'd see three, four or five pieces and know exactly where they fit. *Maddening.* Puzzles are *maddening*.

"How's it coming?" Pam would text me every few days. Occasionally, she'd also send a picture of the lovely five hundred or so piece puzzle she had just completed in, like, two days. "Let me know when you're ready for another one!"

Did I dare give up? Confess I was a puzzle dolt? *No!* I would persevere, not quit, continue (I was getting good at that) to pick up the pieces I'd swept onto the floor in frustration, and repeat to myself, "Puzzling is obviously good for my brain, since you can hardly do this. No, you will not reduce this puzzle dear Pam loaned you to ashes."

Day after day (well, okay, some days I didn't go near that thing) I kept on. The more pieces I got in, the easier it became as there were fewer and fewer pieces to choose from. The pace picked up; my excitement grew. And then *success*! I patted the last piece down and ran triumphantly around the room. I got my camera, snapped that photo, and sent it to Pam with an "I did it!" message. She was so proud of me. She texted back, "Enjoy it for a few days, then when you take it apart and bring it back, I'll loan you another one." Oh, yeah. There was that.

How rewarding that first puzzle experience was, as subsequent ones have been. The satisfaction of working at a difficult task and creating a lovely, fun picture from little bits of cardboard is something only puzzle aficionados understand. Puzzle work mirrors life so very well. All too often, we can't quite figure out how to take life's problems and put them together to create the big picture. God, however, sees it clearly from his perspective.

"Keep at it," his spirit coaches us. "All you see is bits and pieces, but I will help you put it together if you trust me. Little by little. Day by day. Don't worry about all you can't achieve this day, just put together the pieces you can find. I love you. I know it's frustrating, but I also know you can do it. Persevere, and I promise, you will ultimately experience beauty—great beauty—instead of ashes."

Beauty for Ashes

1. Have you ever put together a puzzle? How did it go? Did you find it enjoyable or frustrating? Why do you think you reacted as you did to the experience?

2. Reflect on a "puzzle" in life you have gone through or are going through. What is it? In what ways did it, or is it, challenging you? What beauty did you finally see, or hope to see?

Scripture Reflection: "It is the glory of God to conceal a matter" (Prov. 25:2).

Why, in your opinion, does God frequently and persistently conceal events and information from us?

Prayer Thought: "Lord, thank you for concealing many things from us, for our ways are not your ways, and we can't begin to totally understand and comprehend your mind and plans. Thank you for walking with us day by day as we work to put the puzzle of our lives together to show the world a beautiful picture of you. Amen."

Goin' West

In all things God works for the good of those who love him.

—Romans 8:28

Confession time, and this will shock, absolutely astound, those of you who enjoy reading wild west novels. I do not care for Louis L'Amour books. There, I've said it.

I do not, and I did not several years ago when downsizing to a much smaller home. My husband loved westerns and had discovered over forty matching hard cover L'Amour books at a public library fundraising sale. Of course, he purchased them, brought them home, and thoroughly enjoyed them. Me? I tried, but no success. Unfortunately, there wasn't room in the new, smaller house for many books. Ashes, sorrows, as beloved items simply had to be rehomed or trashed. And thereby hangs the tale!

My church friend Susan, her friend Angie, and I stood leaning against a basement wall taking a break from their selecting and boxing items they were adopting from my home. Tools, canning jars, other assorted "basement storage oriented" items. They were pleased at finding things they could use, and I was pleased to see perfectly good items find someone who appreciated them.

Savoring our mugs of coffee, we amiably chatted. "I have several shelves of books upstairs you might enjoy, Sue," I offered. "They are mostly Christian-oriented, so perhaps you can use them in your Bible studies, or just enjoy them."

"Sounds good. Let's go up and take a look," she replied. "I can always use more books, and when I'm done with them, I try to pass them on to someone else who might enjoy or benefit from them."

"Deal!" I responded, draining my cup. "Now if only I could figure out what to do with my husband's forty-plus Louis L'Amour western novel collection, I'd be all set. My husband loved those books and re-read them constantly. They're in good condition, so I don't want to trash them. I did advertise them for sale, but no one expressed any interest, oddly enough. Hope I can just give them away. I really don't want to throw them out."

Sue's friend Angie gasped and started, literally, hopping up and down in excitement. "Oh my goodness, you won't believe this! Louis L'Amour! And a matched set! Seriously, you are willing to give them away?"

"Well, yes, I am. Uh, are you interested?" I asked, somewhat surprised at her very enthusiastic response.

"Yes, yes, yes!"

Sue and I just stared at her. What in the world?

"I'll take them," she asserted, settling down a bit. "Now, if you'll both help me pack them up and carry them to my car, I'd be so grateful."

"Well, grab a few boxes and let's head upstairs to the living room. But are you sure about this?"

"Yes. Absolutely sure."

As we boxed the books, Angie related this "coincidence" story.

"My dad absolutely loves Louis L'Amour. Anytime he can get downtown to the library, he checks some out. He's probably read every single book more than once but loves to re-read them. I've been thinking that for Christmas, I'd love to buy a few of his favorites for him, so he'd have them in the house when the weather turns bad. His town library is really small, so he often must request the titles he wants, then go back later to pick them up when they come in.

"Now guess what? Thanks to you, I'll be sending him over forty books for Christmas. He won't believe it! Probably have a heart attack in joy. Oh, he'll be *so* excited! I think I'll tuck in a new coffee mug and a pound of his favorite coffee. How I wish I could be there to see his face when the boxes arrive, and he opens them. I'll tell Mom to be sure and video it for me."

Angie paused and sighed happily. "This has to be God's doing. I go to a total stranger's house, looking for nothing in particular. I mostly came to keep Sue company, we're in a basement, and you casually mention the L'Amour books upstairs. If you hadn't, I'd probably never even have noticed a set of brown books particularly. But you did mention it, and I'm here, and oh my goodness."

"You can't be at your dad's house when he opens them? Where does your father live?" I asked. "Perhaps we could help you carry them over to him."

"Seattle. Washington state."

"Seattle!" Sue and I gasped. "Uh, you're going to ship them from North Carolina to Seattle?"

"Sure." Angie shrugged. "I'm getting them for free and shipping will be cheaper than buying this many books new. But more importantly, just imaging my dad's pleasure when he sees them, knowing I made this effort, is priceless."

Sue and I had to agree. What a marvelous gift of not only books, but of love Angie would be giving to her father. And for the three of us to see God so obviously at work in our lives brought praise to our hearts.

My husband's move to assisted living. Downsizing from my home of many years to a smaller place. Life changes and often very trying times. Ashes, ashes, ashes as years of accumulation and memories were sold, set at the curb for adoption, or donated. Tears, fears, uncertainty.

And then, out of the ashes, God's obvious, unexpected, and reassuring presence becomes apparent. "I am here," he reminded. "I am blessing my child Angie through you, and I am blessing you. I, the Lord, work all things for good to those who love me." Amen!

Beauty for Ashes

1. Hopefully, there has been a time in your life when God showed you his presence in a large or small way. What took place? How did it affect you?

2. God works through his people in often unexpected ways. Reflect on a time when God used you to bless and enrich the life of someone else when you least expected it!

Scripture Reflection: "In all things God works for the good of those who love him" (Rom. 8:28).

Does this verse mean everything in a believer's life will in and of itself be good? Why or why not? Can you give biblical support for your thoughts?

Prayer thought: "Lord, while you can and do move mountains, oftentimes you bless us and show your power in small, even easily overlooked ways. I thank you for such unexpected moments, as I can feel you smiling and gently saying, 'Child, I love you.' Thank you, Lord for your grace and goodness. Amen."

Disconnected

Feeling disconnected with me.
For the first time in my life
I am alone, struggling with
Who is left inside.

For the first time
I am alone with me.
I have no clue who "me"
Is supposed to be.

I am still a daughter,
A mother,
A grandmother
But no longer a wife.

I wasn't prepared.
I wasn't ready to be standing here alone.
We were to grow old together
In our little home.

Elizabeth M. Roberts

It's Grand

Then you will call, and the Lord will answer; you
will cry for help, and he will say: Here am I.

—Isaiah 58:9

"Oh my," the music director of a church located two hours away from my home sighed with reverence. "Oh my."

Lying on his stomach on the carpet, his knowledgeable hands examined the pedal assembly, assessing the creaks, groans, and stickiness of each of the three-foot pedals.

"Hum. This will need some work, probably a total replacement set of new ones. I'd say a dog has peed on them more than once."

Ouch. I cringed at the sad truth, and we both stared at my little terrier, who sat looking innocent behind the doggie gate blocking him from the piano room.

"Yea, well," I sighed. "Didn't happen often, and I always cleaned it up as soon as I noticed."

"Yes. Well, ma'am, dog urine and fine pedal mechanisms just don't make a good fit. I will say, the underside of the actual piano looks in top shape."

He crawled out from under my baby grand, taking care not to bump his head. "Okay, let's check the keyboard and look at the strings and felts."

Expert fingers ran up and down the keys, bringing out beautiful sounds I, with my admittedly mediocre talent, was never able to achieve. "Key action is quite good, given the piano's thirty or so years. Good thing your dog is short."

Hahaha, I thought. Yea, well. He did have a point.

"You've taken care of it well. It's in tune. Let's take a look inside." He propped open the lid, turned on his little headlamp, and dove in, so to speak. "Oh my," he sighed contentedly. "These handmade Baldwins from back in the day are works of art. I used to work for Baldwin and in my younger days, I actually helped construct these instruments."

He straightened up and turned to me, his eyes shining. "Never thought I'd lay my hands on one again, and here it is. And it's for sale, and it may end up at my church. Oh my."

He turned to his companion, who was my original contact person from the church. "Take it, absolutely. You'll never have an opportunity like this again. It will be worth every penny."

Turning to me, he continued. "Now, ma'am, realistically we can't offer you top dollar. First off, the church board allocated only so much money to purchase a new piano. Secondly, while you kept it tuned and in reasonable repair, there's the foot pedal assembly issue, plus it needs all new felts and hammers, refinishing where the black paint has flaked off, and replacement of all the string wires. And then we must transport it. Disassemble, truck to the church, which is a distance away, unload and reassemble."

The two men went outside to discuss their best offer while I waited with both hope that my piano would have a super home, and sheer sadness at having to let it go. Upon their return, they named a fair and acceptable price. I said yes, and the deal was done. They were elated with their find; I was relieved. Within a week, the instrument was settled in their church and greatly admired by all who saw and played it.

Beauty from ashes. Ashes? Where were the ashes? My husband's declining health, hospitalization, and two months stay in rehabilitation forced me to face some hard realities. While not upon us yet—he did come home from rehabilitation able to function—the proverbial writing was on the wall. Whether he could stay at home for a while or would need to eventually go to assisted living, downsizing from our large home to a small ranch-style home, or to an apartment, loomed in our future. Looking ahead, there was no place for a grand piano in our plans, and I dreaded the thought of possibly having to move in haste, thereby necessitating hauling it to the landfill or giving it to a thrift store. The time to find a suitable place for it was now, but as I began the search reality hit. Established piano dealers weren't interested in buying a grand piano. The market for them, it turned out, was extremely limited, regardless of the instrument's quality.

I ran ads in newspapers and online. No takers, but the choir director from my church saw one of my posts and referred me to our denomination's region-wide website. Within days, the church two hours away inquired and negotiations began. God's plan for bringing good from the difficult began to fall in place. Their need for a grand piano. Their music director's experience working for Baldwin, and his immediate love for the instrument. The way finding piano movers, loading, and transporting went smoothly. And the success of the restoration, bringing a classic piano back to perfection.

That day, as the truck with my piano inside drove away, I stood watching it go down the road, tears in my eyes. Thirty years of joy, solace, and memories gone; my life situation appearing to be turning into ashes. However, the joy of knowing many people in that church would be praising God in song, accompanied by my beloved instrument, for years to come filled me with tremendous joy. To this day, years later, the incredible converging of God's plan stands as witness to his promise. He does, indeed, bring beauty from ashes.

Beauty from Ashes

1. Letting go. Departing with cherished possessions. Life, which often necessitates change. Select such an event you've experienced, or anticipate experiencing, in your life. What led, or will lead up to it? How did you, or will you, manage it?

2. Sometimes we experience great blessing and joy from someone else's loss, which can feel very awkward. Ponder an occasion when you were able to help, comfort, or assist someone coping with a difficult situation, even though obviously benefiting

yourself. In what way did you realize God was at work in the situation, using you to help them?

Scripture Reflection: "Then you will call, and the Lord will answer; you will cry for help, and he will say: Here am I" (Isa. 58:9).

Does this verse bring you hope and comfort? Have you found it to be true? Why or why not.

Prayer Thought: "Lord, it is when we recognize and acknowledge reality, and are willing to let go and trust you, that unexpected blessings often come. Letting go, however, of beloved possessions and people can be difficult. Be with us, guide us and give us your peace as we cope with life. Amen."

Goodbye

The day I feared,
the day had come
when my stranger had to leave.

The stranger who became
my friend, the best one
I ever had.

I held his hand.
We prayed together,
then said our last goodbyes.

With a quiet
"I'll love your always,"
I stood there by his side.

Elizabeth M. Roberts

Curb Service

Do not store up for yourselves treasures on earth.
—Matthew 6:19

"I really think I'm going crazy! I've got so much stuff in my house, it's depressing. When I try to organize, all I do is move stuff from one room to another," wailed my friend Wanda. That sounds silly, but it's not. It's contributing to my depression and anxiety. I've carried some stuff out to my car, but now my car is packed solid. I need to get to the secondhand store, but I can't seem to get motivated because if I unload everything and come home, I'll just feel like I need to load it up again. Besides, a lot of my stuff is too bulky to get in the car. Guess I need to call a junk removal company, but that might be expensive. Besides, some of my stuff is usable. I hate to just throw everything away.

"Sorry to dump on you. Oops, not the best word to use. Well, maybe it is! Anyway, I just must lament to someone! Maybe I should build a bonfire and just burn all this stuff to ashes, but with my luck, I'd probably burn my house down too." She paused for breath.

Beyond doubt, Wanda was in the throes of an anxiety attack and spinning her mental wheels. However, based on my downsizing experience of a few years ago, I had a plan.

"Wanda, girl, take a deep breath and just listen up here for a few minutes," I instructed. "Let me know when it's okay for me to talk."

We went silent until, after several seconds, she more calmly said, "Okay, I'm better. Ready to listen. What's your thoughts?"

"Remember several years ago, when I had to downsize from my big house to my little place?"

"Oh yeah," she said. "I don't know how in the world you did it. Especially now that I'm trying to thin stuff out, I can really appreciate all the decisions you had to…"

"Whoa again. Stop. Calm down. Breath. Now just listen a bit here," I instructed. "Here's what worked for me, and maybe it will for you because you live in a similar neighborhood, where people walk and drive down the streets."

"True. Have a lot of folks that walk and stuff," she agreed.

"So here's what just might help you find homes for at least some of your stuff. Set it in your yard, near the curb. If you want, you can even put a 'free' sign on it."

"Uh, but lots of it's junky or doesn't work."

"No matter. Put it out there and give it a try. I could not believe how many of my cast-off items were someone else's treasure! Please, just try it, okay?"

She sighed, clearly doubtful. "Well, guess I could put a few things out, like my old gas push mower and those rusty garden tools that have been around forever. Got some scratched old end tables, and there's a dog crate I don't need anymore."

"Super. Try it. Keep me posted," I encouraged.

Wasn't but a few days or so and Wanda showed up on my doorstep. "Got a minute?" she said. "I just gotta share. It's been amazing."

Over cookies and coffee, she related her tale. "Okay, so after our talk the other day, I dragged that old mower to the curb, along with the rusty tools, the dog crate, and a bunch of other bulky stuff. Well, wasn't but a few hours after and this young man came to the door, asking if he could take the mower! I told him it didn't work, but he said he was a whiz at fixing mowers, and he could really use it because he had started a lawn maintenance business and needed equipment. Happily, he loaded it up, along with the tools.

"Before I knew it, when I looked out, the chipped and scratched end tables were gone, as was the dog crate, and most amazingly a big box of old VHS tapes. I mean, who even has a VHS player now days! When I hauled more stuff out to the curb, within days it all disappeared. Even an old, scratched bunk bed frame. It was adopted by a young mom who asked me if I could hold it for her until her friend with a pickup truck could come get it. When I told her it needed repair, she said no problem. She'd do it because it would be a blessing that her two young boys wouldn't have to sleep on mattresses on the floor. When she came back, I threw in a bunch of blankets, sheets, and pillows I didn't need also.

"It's just been amazing. To think I was hoarding all that stuff and other people could have been using it. I'm so ashamed, but I'm turning over a new leaf here. Pray for me. It's still hard to let go of perfectly good stuff, even though I never use it. God's just been opening my eyes!"

Wanda and I finished our visit by discussing how the Lord works through his people to bless others. He seems to like working through us, in order to clearly demonstrate how old, broken things, including people, can be redeemed. He is the master at giving beauty for ashes.

Beauty for Ashes

1. Reflect on, or share a time, when something you considered trash turned out to be greatly appreciated by another person. How did it come about? What was your reaction when you realized how much it meant to them?

2. On the other hand, has there been a time when you benefited from someone else's cast-offs? How did it come about? Why was it such a blessing to you?

Scripture Reflection: "Do not store up for yourselves treasures on earth" (Matt. 6:19).

Is God saying we should not own anything? If not, what do you think this verse is teaching us? Looking up Matthew 6 and reading the context might be helpful.

Prayer thought: "Our Father, we thank you for supplying our needs in so many ways. Forgive us, however, when we become greedy and won't 'let go' of material things, thereby demonstrating a possible lack of trust in you. Thank you for partnering with us, if we are willing, to supply the needs of others. Amen."

Squishy, Squishy.
Mush. Mush. Mush.

No good tree bears bad fruit. Nor does a bad tree bear
good fruit. Each tree is recognized by its own fruit.
—Luke 6:43–45

"Hey, God! I am ready to start helping you out by volunteering. Yes, I had some big life changes and had to back off on things for a while, and the COVID-19 lockdowns sure did not help. But as you know, Father, I'm recovering and lockdowns have eased, as long as we follow precautions. So let me at 'em!"

Well, how fortuitous. Come the next Sunday, a dear sister-in-Christ sitting down the row from me unexpectedly leaned over and said, "If you have some time, the community food pantry really could use more volunteers. Things are picking back up, donations are coming in, so think about it, okay?"

I can take a hint. Within days, I contacted the director with my eager offer to lend a hand. Given my extensive educational qualifications, teaching background, and English skills, I anticipated working the intake desk, doing counseling with clients, or some sort of publicity/record-keeping work. I would be a natural! So when the email arrived instructing me to show up at nine forty-five the following Tuesday morning, I was excited and ready to go. "Wear casual clothes," it instructed. Sounds good; I will not have to dress up any. Jeans and a nice shirt should do it.

Tuesday, at nine forty-five, and here I am. Here the director is. Here a long white folding table is, all set up. Here are several stacks of large produce boxes, some of which seem to be oozing liquid. Here under the table are empty boxes.

"Here are your plastic gloves," the lady in charge said, "and there are more in the cupboard over here, if you need them. Be sure to always wear your plastic gloves."

"Heads up!" she said as she smacked a big box down on the table in front of me. "Rotten and bad produce go in the trash boxes under the table. The farmers pick them up tomorrow for pig feed. Good, edible fruits go on the rolling wire racks there at the end of the table. Edible veggies go into the designated bins on the rolling carts behind me here. Use your own judgment."

"Yes, ma'am," I said, gazing at the box of donated fruit from a local grocery store. "These bags of grapes look promising," I thought, lifting them from the box and turning them over. Oops. Right many of them seem to be wearing little fuzzy jackets, sort of white and greenish in color. Garbage box. Yuck. Okay, a layer of avocados. I love avocados! Pick them out and put them onto the good to go cart…oops. Squish. Mush in my hands. They seem to be a tad over-ripe. The reason for the plastic gloves rule is becoming evident.

Well, out of that big box, there were some nice oranges, apples, and grapes. Glancing under the table, I could only think the pig farmers were going to be happy. Okay. Now to tackle the box of veggies she next positioned on the table. Bagged salads. Top layer here looks to be pretty nice. They are not even out of date! Nice bunches of collard and mustard greens. Check. Caesar salad in bags looks decent. Put neatly on client cart.

Next layer coming up and glory be, it is a miracle! Lettuce and such have transformed themselves inside the plastic bags into what I guess could be labeled "vegetable broth." Deadly vegetable broth, undoubtedly, but interesting. Kinda black and stinky. Gross, actually. I shall never eat a bagged salad again in my life. Never. Squish, mush, slime. "We need more garbage boxes," I informed my leader. And so it went, as my education continued.

I have learned much over the past weeks about fruits and vegetables. Starfruit does not twinkle after a certain point. Pineapples truly pine when overly ripe. There's onion smell and then there is *rotten* onion smell. Do not even need to do a close inspection on beyond-their-prime potatoes. And always there are enough rotten tomatoes to throw at endless numbers of horrible stage actors or crooked politicians.

We really have interesting times when young teenage boys occasionally come to help, doing community service for school or scouts. You can imagine the fun they have. "No," my leader firmly states, "you can*not* throw rotten bananas at your friend. Stop it right now."

Of course, shouts of "Oh, gross!" and "Whew. Look at *this*!" fill the air.

And there we are, week after week. I am getting skilled at this, and my executive decision-making skills have stood me in good stead. All those years working with students have helped me spot the rotten apples in a heartbeat. Seriously, the interesting part of the experience has been how much I actually enjoy my task. It is not glamorous, high-powered, or flashy. However, it is necessary. For from the piles of decay, I and my fellow workers extract wholesome, edible, perfect vegetables, and fruits to trolley out to the client distribution area, where people in need can select what they need to make wholesome meals for their families. A true blessing, indeed.

Beauty from Ashes

Working the produce sorting area provides a perfect example of how God sorts through the "ashes," the decay and waste of our lives, and plucks out the good things that lie within us. Without his discerning love, our decay would continue unabated until we became totally rotten and unredeemable. Through Jesus, however, beauty hidden in the mess is brought forth and displayed in our lives for all to see and benefit from.

1. Do you have stories from your own life that deal with good coming from what appears to be something totally worthless? What was the situation? How did God bring forth the good?

2. Think of a time when you volunteered or worked in an unpleasant, perhaps unappreciated situation, and you found to your surprise you actually derived great satisfaction from your nasty task. What do you think brought that joy forth?

Scripture Study: "No good tree bears bad fruit. Nor does a bad tree bear good fruit. Each tree is recognized by its own fruit" (Luke 6:43–44).

Obviously, this verse is stating a truth about literal trees, but what is the deeper application or message it is saying about our lives in Christ?

Prayer thought: "Lord, let me live in such a way that good fruit springs forth from my life, so others can clearly see I am rooted and grafted in you. Take away that which is rotten, that which hampers my ability to witness to others of your goodness through my actions. Thank you, Lord. Amen."

Why Fear?

Why fear about tomorrow
for God's already there.
Why worry about the sorrow
for you have God's love and care.

No amount of worry
will take away the fear.
So don't worry about tomorrow
for God holds you near.

He takes away the worry.
He takes away the fear.
So hold onto tomorrow
for God's already there.

Elizabeth Roberts

Beauty for Ashes

It is finished.

—John 19:30

It appeared to be finished. Over. No hope remaining. All their dreams totally dashed to pieces as their Hope, their Messiah, hung on a Roman cross. Suffering. Bleeding. Dying. Thorns piercing his skulk. Spear wound in his side. Nails in his hands and feet. The women stood weeping, watching.

All the beautiful words and promises seemingly nothing but empty promises and fine rhetoric. What was the point of all the past years? What was the point of the miracles of healing, raising people from the dead, casting out demons, and gaining followers? Was it all for *this*? A nasty day on a nasty hill among nasty, supposedly religious people, nasty Roman soldiers gambling for the clothes of the dying at the foot of the nasty cross. It simply made no sense whatsoever.

His opponents rubbed their hands in glee, cackling "He saved others, but he can't save himself. He's the king of Israel!" (Matt. 27:42).

Darkness, an eerie unnatural darkness, fell over the whole land from noon until three o'clock. The dying man cried out in anguish to God. Then, Jesus was clearly dead between the two dying thieves hanging on crosses on either side of him. He, himself, had announced death was settling in on him, as he called out, quoting Psalm 31:5, "Into your hands I commit my spirit" (Luke 23:46). Life left him as his body slumped, pulling down on the nails in his hands.

Soldiers gambled at the foot of the crosses, hot, tired, and bored by the bloody business. Jesus's robe was exquisite, woven seamlessly in one piece by loving hands, so instead of tearing it to divide among themselves, they let winner take all as they rolled the dices.

Darkness came, literally and figuratively. Some loyal women and men huddled nearby, though most of his followers and friends were safely hidden away. What thoughts were in the minds of those observers? What greater ashes could there be than the total dashing of years of rising hopes that here, then, was the Messiah, the healer, of Israel and all the world. He had often performed deeds exhibiting great power on his part. Rebuking stormy seas. Casting out demons and healing the insane. Boldly clearing the great temple of God by fearlessly driving out those buying and selling for corrupt profit. He wasn't afraid. He wasn't timid. He stood up to those opposing him and God's words.

Until he didn't. What were they to make of it? His followers were with him in the Garden of Gethsemane. They even had a weapon or two, and Peter actually slashed out with a sword, trying to defend Jesus. Except, Jesus rebuked him and healed the wounded servant of the enemy. How did that make any sense? Had Jesus lost his sanity? What was going on?

Truth is, Jesus had explained many things to his followers about this troubled time. That he would be taken, he would die, he would rise again, but they, being human, for the most part became overwhelmed by fear and emotions to the point where logical thought and memory fled. Most of us have "been there, done that," in times of great disaster or stress. And so, in the garden of their overwhelming confusion and dread, the disciples simply ran for their lives. Perhaps they assumed Jesus was well able to take care of himself, based on past experiences, so they didn't even look back to see what was happening.

And Jesus was led off to an illegal trial full of cruelty, mockery, and hatred. Were those persecuting and tormenting him perhaps a bit confused, themselves, at his extraordinary meekness. This man who had thundered and stood firm, now meek as a lamb facing slaughter? Was their moment of triumph so great, that it didn't cross their minds to wonder, "What's going on here?"

Jesus was taken off the cross, wrapped up, and laid to rest in the tomb of a friend. Hidden away in a cave-like edifice, resting. Friends wept, and then left in sorrow to comfort one another and try to make some sense of it all. Ashes, ashes, ashes. All their dreams dashed and destroyed. Ugliness everywhere. Despair and doom. The light had gone out.

And then…

What is this radiance from these angelic-looking beings at the tomb? What are they saying? "He is not here; he has risen, just as he said. Come and see the place where he lay" (Matt. 28:6).

They saw him. The women saw him. Many of the disciples saw him. Several times. Walking, talking, eating, praying, teaching. They saw the unbelievable radiance of the Light of the World that will never, ever, be quenched by evil. Glorious. Beautiful. Beauty. Beauty. Beauty. Eternal, everlasting Beauty.

"He bestowed on them a crown of beauty instead of ashes, the oil of joy instead of mourning, and a garment of praise instead of a spirit of despair" (Isa. 61:3).

Beauty for Ashes

1. From Jesus's sacrificial death comes life for all those who believe in him and accept him as savior, humbly admitting our short-comings and seeking to rely on his grace. "For by grace you have been saved through faith—and this is not from yourselves; it is the gift of God—not by works, so that no one may boast" (Eph. 2:8–9). Have you asked Jesus to take over your life? If not, write a simple request for him to save you now.

2. As you ponder the death and resurrection of Jesus the Christ, jot down what thoughts fill your heart and mind.

Scripture Reflection*:* "It is finished" (John 19:30).

Three words. What, to you, makes this simple sentence so eternally powerful.

Prayer Thought: "Great and mighty God of all creation, what are we humans, that you are mindful of us or care about us in the least? Your efforts to redeem us, if we are but willing, defy our understanding, but we are more grateful than we can being to express. Thank you for allowing us to fellowship with you. Amen."

About the Authors

Sandra R. Still

Sandra's previous books include *I Can't Fix It But I Know Who Can*, which focuses on struggling people seeking hope, joy, and comfort, and *Out on a Ledge and Other Teachable Moments*, which recounts inspiring and challenging incidents from her thirty-plus years in public high school classrooms. Her latest work, *Ashes in the Closet*, examines how God fulfills his promise to give us beauty for ashes as we go through life. While all things are not good of themselves, God promises to work all things for good to those who love him.

A National Board–certified teacher, Sandra holds a MEd in counseling and a BS in education. A commissioned Stephen Minister, she lives with her Dandie Dinmont terrier, Calvin, in Garner, North Carolina.

Elizabeth M. Roberts

"My poems are pure emotion and crying of the heart to God, like many of King David's psalms were as he went through life's trials," explains Elizabeth.

Faced over the years with life situations familiar to us all—dark times, loneliness, strained relationships, deaths—talking to God through poetry became her solace. Now, she gives God praise and shares her work in hopes of encouraging and comforting others.

A lover of travel, Elizabeth especially enjoys taking the train. She has "ridden the rails" from North Carolina across the nation to Oregon. When at home, church activities, her children, and grandchildren, keep her busy and involved. She resides in Valparaiso, Indiana, with several clever, amusing, and well-loved cats.